Hunting Down the Terrorists

Declaring War and Policing Global Violations

Hunting Down the Terrorists

Declaring War and Policing Global Violations

THE
LUCENT
LIBRARY OF
HOMELAND
SECURITY

Hunting Down the Terrorists

Declaring War and Policing Global Violations

Laurel Corona

Mishawaka-Penn-Harris
Public Library
Mishawaka, Indiana

**LUCENT
BOOKS®**

THOMSON

GALE

San Diego • Detroit • New York • San Francisco • Cleveland • New Haven, Conn. • Waterville, Maine • London • Munich

© 2004 by Lucent Books. Lucent Books is an imprint of The Gale Group, Inc.,
a division of Thomson Learning, Inc.

Lucent Books® and Thomson Learning™ are trademarks used herein under license.

For more information, contact
Lucent Books
27500 Drake Rd.
Farmington Hills, MI 48331-3535
Or you can visit our Internet site at http://www.gale.com

LIBRARY OF CONGRESS CATALOGING-IN-PUBLICATION DATA

Corona, Laurel, 1949–
   Hunting down the terrorists: declaring war and policing global violations / by Laurel Corona.
     p. cm. — (The Lucent library of homeland security)
Summary: Discusses the "international war on terror" which was begun in the aftermath of
the September 11, 2001, attacks, including military, technological, economic, and other
weapons being employed.
Includes bibliographical references.
   ISBN 1-59018–382–7 (hardback : alk. paper)
   1. War on Terrorism, 2001– —Juvenile literature. [1. War on Terrorism, 2001– 2. Terrorists.]
I. Title. II. Series.
   HV6431.C67 2004
   973.931—dc22
                                    2003014084

Printed in the United States of America

Contents

Foreword

Stunned by the terrorist attacks of September 11, 2001, millions of Americans clung to President George W. Bush's advice in a September 20 live broadcast speech to "live your lives, and hug your children." His soothing words made an indelible impression on people in need of comfort and paralyzed by fear. Recent history had seen no greater emotional flood than occurred in the days following September 11, as people were united by deep shock and grief and an instinctive need to feel safe.

Searching for safety, a panicked nation urged taking extreme and even absurd measures. Immediately after the attacks, it was suggested that all aircraft passengers be restrained for the duration of flights—better to restrict the movement of all than to risk allowing one dangerous passenger to act. After the attempted bombing of a flight from Paris to Atlanta in December 2001, one *New York Times* columnist even half-seriously suggested starting an airline called Naked Air—"where the only thing you wear is a seat belt." Although such acute fear and paranoia waned as the attacks slipped further into the past, a dulled but enduring desire to overhaul national security remained.

Creating the Department of Homeland Security was one way to allay citizens' panic and fear. Congress has allocated billions to secure the nation's infrastructure, bolster communication channels, and protect precious monuments against terrorist attack. Further funding has equipped emergency responders with state-of-the-art tools such as hazardous-material suits and networked communication systems. Improved databases and intelligence-gathering tools have extended the reach of intelligence agencies, in the effort to ferret out the terrorists hiding among us. Supporters of these programs praised the Bush administration for its attention to security lapses and agreed that in the post–September 11 world, only with tighter security could Americans go about their lives free of fear and reservation.

It did not take long, however, for the sense of national unity and purpose to splinter as people advanced countless ideas for actually achieving that security. As it became evident that ensuring safety meant curtailing Americans' freedom, the price of security became a hotly debated issue. With September 11 now years in the past, and after new wars and aggression waged in its name, it is not clear that the United States is any closer to becoming what many consider impossible: an America immune to attack. As distinguished political science professor Janice Gross Stein maintains, "Military preeminence, no matter how overwhelming, does not buy the United States security from attack, even in its heartland." Whether the invasion of sovereign nations, the deaths of thousands of civilians, and the continued endangerment of American troops have made the world any safer or the United States any less vulnerable to terror is unproved.

All Americans want to feel safe; beyond that basic agreement, however, commonality ends. Thus, how to ensure homeland security, and a myriad of related questions, is one of the most compelling and controversial issues in recent history. The books in this series explore this new chapter in history and examine its successes and challenges. Annotated bibliographies provide readers with ideas for further research, while fully documented primary and secondary source quotations enhance the text. Each book in the series carefully considers a different aspect of homeland security; together they provide students with a wealth of information as well as launching points for further study and discussion.

A War Without Borders

On September 20, 2001, President George W. Bush declared to a joint session of Congress that "the enemies of freedom committed an act of war against our country" and that the United States would "direct every resource at our command—every means of diplomacy, every tool of intelligence, every instrument of law enforcement, every financial influence and every necessary weapon of war—to the disruption and to the defeat of the global terror network." [1] With these words, President Bush introduced to the American people and the world the idea of an international war on terror.

It would clearly be a very different kind of war. For centuries the idea of war had been relatively well defined: One country or coalition of countries attacked another by armed force and the attacked country reacted militarily. Some wars were limited or localized; other conflicts involved mass destruction and much of the world. All traditional wars, however, shared a basic aspect: They were waged by nations over territory and power. In the aftermath of the destruction of the World Trade Center and the attack on the Pentagon on September 11, 2001, it quickly became apparent how much the world had changed, and how untraditional the war against terrorism would be.

No formal government or army had mounted the September 11 attack. No territory was seized or lost. If a war was to be declared, which country would be the enemy? At what point could the war be declared won or lost? These are legitimate questions to ask when a country goes to war, but in this case, if there were answers, they were not obvious or easy ones. The newly declared global war on terror would not be against a conventional enemy and would not in the end be judged a success or failure by where lines on a map were drawn at the end of the conflict.

Rather than a nation, the enemy was a group of people who sought to harm the United States and its people by any means. They did not wear uniforms or form armies. Some were centered in organized terrorist camps in so-called sponsor nations such as Libya, Sudan, and Afghanistan, while others trained and lived in small groups known as cells in neighborhoods scattered around the world. Some were known to U.S.

Shortly after the terrorist attacks of September 11, 2001, President George W. Bush condemns terrorism during a speech at California's Travis Air Force Base.

government intelligence agencies, while others lived anonymously and unsuspected. The ease of international travel and movement of foreigners into and out of the United States contributed to a growing realization that terrorists could truly be anywhere at any time, free to pursue the most devastating plans. To deal with them, new tactics and strategies, as well as new forms of diplomacy and international cooperation, would be required.

The U.S. Response to International Terrorism Before September 11

Long before September 11, 2001, foreign terrorists, particularly radical Islamic terrorists, had attacked American interests at home and abroad, and the United States had reacted

strongly. For example, when the American embassies in Kenya and Tanzania were attacked by terrorists in 1998, President Bill Clinton ordered bombings of known terrorist training camps in Sudan and Afghanistan. The actions of the United States at that time were a preview of the new kind of war President Bush would declare three years later.

The Clinton administration felt that these exchanges of blows with terrorist groups in the 1990s were necessary to keep terrorism under control, but in reality a backlash against the United States was gathering momentum in much of the Muslim world. Political and individual support for Osama bin Laden and his al-Qaeda organization, as well as for other terrorist groups, grew along with resentment of the ways the United States exercised power around the world. Underestimating this anti-American sentiment, the CIA and other government experts saw events such as the bombing of the USS *Cole* in Yemen on October 12, 2000, which killed seventeen and injured thirty-nine, as isolated acts and not as part of an effective confederation of terrorists bent on targeting the United States.

Declaring a War on Terror

The destruction of the World Trade Center and the attack on the Pentagon on September 11, quickly recognized as the acts of a sophisticated, powerful enemy, were thus a severe shock to the American government. In declaring the war on terror, newly elected president George W. Bush stated bluntly that any nation that was not "with [the United States]" was "with the terrorists." From that point forward, he said, "any nation that continues to harbor or support terrorism will be regarded by the United States as a hostile regime."[2] To emphasize the point, he ordered the military invasion of Afghanistan to topple the ruling Taliban government, which had provided safe haven for al-Qaeda.

In addition to fighting al-Qaeda in Afghanistan, the United States began stepping up its efforts to root out terrorists elsewhere. These efforts have involved direct military action as well as covert operations to infiltrate and disable terrorist networks.

They require extensive cooperation between nations, including the highly unusual new tactic of sharing intelligence with countries such as Russia, which the United States used to spy against. They involve development of new technologies to identify terrorists and track their movements, as well as use of more established technologies such as satellite tracking and wiretapping.

Elusive Enemy, Elusive Victory

Traditionally, when military forces either conquer a country or make such a conquest clearly inevitable, a surrender or truce ensues, victory is declared, bloodshed ceases, and life returns to normal. Such expectations are unrealistic today because the war is against a different kind of enemy. Even when a nation can be identified as an enemy state, as happened in 2001 in Afghanistan and in 2003 in Iraq, toppling its government does not resolve the larger conflict—world terrorism—which goes on despite even the most complete military victory. Terrorists may be put on the run, but they can regroup in new places. The military defeat of one country or another is likely to create only temporary setbacks for well-funded and widely connected terrorist networks.

The question thus has become how to wage a war in which victory may never be decisively declared. Not until the middle of 2003, for example, did the United States declare the hostilities in Afghanistan, begun in 2001, officially over, and deadly skirmishes continue to occur between American forces and Taliban loyalists. The United States continues to keep troops in Afghanistan to support President Hamid Karzai's efforts to prevent full-scale civil war in his fractured country. The situation in Afghanistan shows that even a successful war against another country seems only a small, temporary, and incomplete victory in the war on terrorism, which some fear may come to resemble what author Gore Vidal has described as "perpetual war for perpetual peace."[3]

The problem with this concept is that it puts the United States in an ongoing struggle with other countries over the legitimacy of its use of force to combat terrorism around the world. The conflict between the United States and most of the rest of the world in 2003 over declaring war on Iraq as part of a larger war on terrorism has had a clear impact on international relations that will be felt for years to come. Multinational commitment to tracking down and neutralizing individual terrorists and their networks is clearly of great importance for the future of humanity, but what the Bush administration has seen

U.S. Marines give water to an Iraqi soldier in 2003. Although U.S. forces succeeded in toppling Saddam Hussein's government, the war on terrorism continues.

as courageous willingness to take the first step to confront terrorism, much of the rest of the world has seen as harmful bullying not likely to improve the overall situation.

Supporters of American intervention in foreign countries, military and otherwise, argue that the end result will be a more peaceful world and a safer America. Critics argue, however, that enforcing American will on sovereign nations will only make the United States more hated and spawn more terrorists with bigger ideas about how to do harm. It remains to be seen whether America's actions will truly result in a more peaceful, or safer world.

Not since the Cold War has the future of the planet seemed to hang on each new political crisis between the United States and its declared enemy. This is indeed a war as significant as any other global war in history. But the world is coming to realize that terror of the sort being waged today may never be eradicated because there will always be people willing to die for a powerful cause. President Bush told the American people shortly after the events of September 11 that they "should not expect one battle, but a lengthy campaign, unlike any other we have ever seen."[4] It is indeed unlike any past war in which adversaries are drawn into showdown battles. It is in fact the opposite. It is a war to ensure that nothing happens at all.

Chapter One

The Role of the Military

In the first days after September 11, it was clear that the war on terror would be conventional in at least one way: U.S. military force would be involved. Stating that there would be no higher foreign policy priority for his administration, President George W. Bush introduced a new policy of pre-emptive military strikes on countries capable of and interested in harming the United States. This doctrine defined capability and intention to harm the United States as reason enough to justify a U.S. attack. Three of the goals of this doctrine are to destroy centers of terrorist operations, to capture the terrorists themselves, and to remove governments whose support of terrorism is considered a threat.

The first test of the doctrine was in 2001 in Afghanistan, where the United States brought together an international military coalition to seek out and destroy al-Qaeda training camps and capture its leaders. The military campaign also toppled Afghanistan's ruling Taliban regime, which had provided the terrorists with a haven. A fuller application of the Bush doctrine came a year and a half later, in the spring of 2003, when approximately three hundred thousand American soldiers were deployed to Iraq to depose its dictator, Saddam Hussein. Like terrorists, Saddam Hussein himself was viewed as a threat that had to be hunted down and destroyed.

In both Afghanistan and Iraq, military victory was swift, but as yet goals have not been completely met. Although

Young U.S. Marines train for a mission in Afghanistan aboard the USS *Bataan*.

governments have been toppled and terrorist centers of operation have been largely destroyed, terrorists remain on the loose, including the undisputed symbolic head of world terrorism, Osama bin Laden. Military strikes, the ongoing search for terrorists and their weapons, and continued American military occupation of targeted countries are clear indications of the importance of the U.S. armed forces in what is expected to be a prolonged and complex war on terrorism around the world.

Bombs and Troops

Though to date only two countries have been the targets of the new Bush doctrine in the war on terror, a pattern has emerged as to how the military will be used. The first stage is a bombing campaign. In Afghanistan, bombs began to fall on October 7, 2001, focusing on al-Qaeda and Taliban strongholds. These assaults involved bombs dropped by aircraft including fighters, bombers, and even helicopters; guided missiles; and artillery shells. Soon soldiers and other military personnel from the United States and other coalition members such as Turkey, Germany, Canada, and Great Britain arrived to hunt terrorists hiding deep in the remote mountains of eastern Afghanistan. Ground troops quelled active resistance by shelling positions, cutting off supply routes, and apprehending those in the area thought to be assisting terrorists. Once an area was captured, troops combed the site for useful evidence and arrested anyone still there.

By the end of 2001, the Taliban had been uprooted, and a new interim government friendlier to the United States was in place. Al-Qaeda had retreated to what seemed to be its last base in Afghanistan, on the Pakistan border, near Jalalabad, an area journalist Johanna McGeary calls "the famously impregnable eastern Afghanistan cave complex called Tora Bora."[5] Because the area is so remote and the terrain is so rough, the Tora Bora caves are difficult to reach even on foot. For this reason, U.S. military planners decided that intensive bombing raids of the region would be the most effective way to go after the terrorists. "Our specialized approach is to put 500-lb. bombs in the entrances"[6] of the caves, marine general Peter Pace, vice chairman of the Joint Chiefs of Staff, said at the early stages of the campaign. At first bombings were effective in flushing out or killing terrorists, but eventually it became clear that enemy fighters within reach of the bombs had either been killed or evacuated, and the focus shifted to methodical cave-by-cave searches.

Searching the caves was a cooperative effort between Afghan and coalition troops, but the use of American soldiers was actually quite limited. The U.S. military leadership, under the field command of General Tommy Franks, decided not to risk American lives in the initial stages of the search. Instead, while the possibility remained strong that armed combatants might still be in the caves or waiting to ambush the searchers, the

An Afghan guerrilla fighter guards the entrance to one of the caves of the al-Qaeda base in Tora Bora.

sweeps were conducted by Afghans, who knew the area—and presumably the likely tactics of the terrorists—better. After this step, American soldiers and Special Forces operatives took inventories of what was in the caves and ensured no terrorists remained there.

This strategy, though it is likely to have saved some American lives, was later felt to be a mistake by some military leaders on the scene, because the Afghans hired by the United States to clear the caves of potential combatants had no particular loyalty to the United States and its objectives. Many terrorists, possibly including bin Laden and Taliban leader Mullah Omar, escaped with the direct assistance, or at least under the less than watchful eye, of the Afghan search parties. "All of this . . . got us nothing. No weapons, no ammo, no nothing,"[7] General Tommy Franks, the disgruntled military commander later said. By early 2002 it seemed clear that few if any Taliban and al-Qaeda leaders remained in Afghanistan.

The military effort was generally seen as a qualified success. A number of Taliban and al-Qaeda leaders had been killed or captured, including key lieutenants of Mullah Omar and Osama bin Laden. Many lower-ranking terrorists were rounded up and put in prison camps first in Afghanistan and later at the U.S. naval base at Guantánamo Bay, Cuba. However, both bin Laden and Mullah Omar eluded death or capture during the bombardment and search, possibly by crossing the border into Pakistan. Eventually the military effort in Afghanistan became centered not so much on making headline-grabbing arrests of major al-Qaeda leaders but on routine military patrols, primarily along the mountainous border with Pakistan, as well as covert activities by small units of Special Forces officers.

New Focus, Old Strategy

By 2002 the focus of the war on terror had shifted away from Afghanistan onto Iraq and its leader, Saddam Hussein. Citing what it claimed was concrete and indisputable evidence that

Saddam had weapons of mass destruction and was linked to the events of September 11, the United States went to war, along with its ally Great Britain to overthrow the Iraqi regime and find and destroy these weapons.

Operation Iraqi Freedom, as this new military offensive was called, followed the same strategy that had been used in Afghanistan. Heavy bombing pounded the country, particularly its capital, Baghdad. Soon after, U.S. and British forces crossed the border and began advancing on the capital. As in Afghanistan, the Iraqi government fell quickly, but also as in Afghanistan, Iraq's top leaders, including Saddam and his two sons, were not killed or captured. They simply disappeared, leaving it unclear whether they were dead or alive. This took away a sense of completeness from the victory and once again led to the uneasy conclusion that the war on terror was going to have few clear and complete victories.

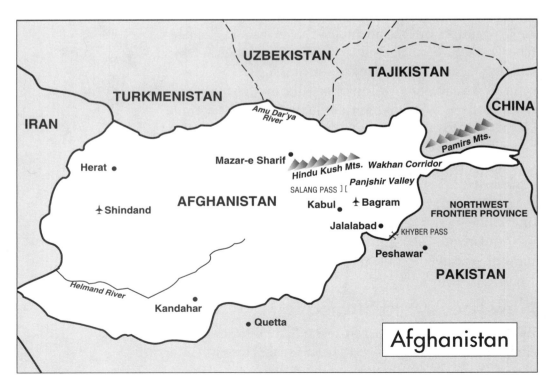

U.S. military personnel attach a Special Forces vehicle to a helicopter for transport to Afghanistan.

Searching for Terrorists While Keeping the Peace

Conventionally, when the purpose of a war has been in part to overthrow the government of a foreign country, the victorious armies withdraw after conflict, leaving behind a small occupation force to ensure law and order temporarily while a new government takes shape. In Iraq and Afghanistan that process is complicated by the continuing presence of fighting units that have stayed behind to search for any terrorists that may be on the run. Both of these large countries offer countless hiding places for terrorists, including not only remote mountains and small desert villages, but also big-city shelter, among sympathizers with their cause.

The postwar occupation of Afghanistan is also complicated because not long after the election of Hamid Karzai as president, it became clear that law and order would not come easily to this country. One source of the problem is the cultivation of opium, from which heroin is processed, and its export around the world. Afghanistan is the world's largest opium producer, and many powerful people in Afghanistan have become enormously wealthy by exploiting this crop. Because drug production and distribution is not only illegal but also very disruptive to the smooth and peaceful functioning of a country, within Afghanistan another bloody conflict has ensued between the Karzai government and those involved with the opium trade. This includes not only terrorist groups using drug money to fund activities around the world, but also corrupt tribal leaders within Afghanistan itself.

Throughout Afghanistan's history, the region has been controlled by tribal warlords who have maintained immense power and control even when a central government has been in place. In the aftermath of the fall of the Taliban, warlords quickly began looking for opportunities to increase their individual authority. In this climate, warlords are more likely to make deals with each other against the Karzai government and also cooperate with terrorists, especially when doing so might increase their wealth as well as their power.

Such shifting alliances among warlords and terrorists further complicate U.S. efforts to stablilize the country. The ability of warlords to disrupt Afghan-American attempts to rid the country of terrorists has already been illustrated. For example, in December 2001 a convoy of local tribal leaders

Afghan president Hamid Karzai (right) and General Abdul Rashid Dostum attend the first official celebration of the Afghan new year since the fall of the Taliban.

on its way to Karzai's inauguration was demolished by an American bomber, killing sixty-five people. At first U.S. military officials claimed that the bombing was in response to a surface-to-air missile fired from the convoy, but the attack was probably based on bad intelligence. "One competitor may be trying to use our capability for his own benefit,"[8] Rear Admiral John Stufflebeem admitted later, when it was pointed out that the likely culprit was a local warlord who

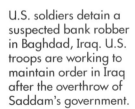

U.S. soldiers detain a suspected bank robber in Baghdad, Iraq. U.S. troops are working to maintain order in Iraq after the overthrow of Saddam's government.

had used the military to wipe out most of his rivals. Karzai himself has narrowly escaped several assassination attempts, and many observers question whether he indeed has any real control of the country outside of the heavily militarized capital of Kabul.

In this climate, it has become increasingly apparent that the United States cannot easily withdraw from Afghanistan without bringing on a collapse of the Karzai government and a return to the conditions that produced the Taliban and its support of terrorism in the first place. This situation reinforces the common belief that an unavoidable component of the war on terror will be long military occupations, at great expense to the American economy and at great risk of American lives. This produces a serious dilemma: If the United States leaves Afghanistan, what was gained by going to war in the first place is likely to be lost. However, the longer the United States stays, the greater the potential is for cultivating a new generation of terrorists, motivated by resentment of the occupation.

Hunting Down Terrorists in Postwar Iraq

A similar situation is evolving in Iraq. Despite Saddam Hussein's brutality, his regime did enforce law and order in Iraq. Since the fall of the Saddam regime, American troops are engaged in the difficult effort to keep order while Iraq forms a new government and people adjust to life without Saddam. In part because of Saddam's refusal to surrender, the damage done to the country by bombs and destruction of essential services was extensive. Especially in the capital, Baghdad, the rubble left behind in the wake of bombings, the breakdown of the ability of the police to maintain order, and the continuing lack of basic services such as electricity and water, has led to a dangerous and chaotic situation.

Many ordinary Iraqi citizens resented the invading Americans, and angry demonstrations and demands that the United States leave the country made it also difficult for

American troops to regain control. Efforts to maintain law and order in a very volatile country are likely to create much more stressful and potentially violent interactions between Iraqis and the occupying American and British forces. Such a situation only serves to underscore the complexities of using military force in the war on terror. Because its resources are so vast, and its capabilities are so great, the military is the source of some of the most noted successes in the war on terror. It also has the greatest potential for backfire and backlash. Despite the risks, the military is likely to stay in Iraq for some time to come, precisely because continued chaos would make it easy for terrorist groups to return. Thus, the United States will continue to keep watch in Iraq that al-Qaeda and other groups do not strengthen themselves there.

The "Axis of Evil" and Beyond

The war on terror has already taken the U.S. military to Afghanistan and Iraq, and other places thought to be connected with terror networks are likely future targets. Before the war in Iraq, President Bush spoke of an "axis of evil,"[9] three countries he identified as the prime obstacles to world peace and the end of terrorism. The three countries were Iraq, Iran, and North Korea. Among other purposes, the war in Iraq served to show the world that Bush intended to keep his promise to go after countries that were deemed hostile. Now that the regime of Saddam Hussein has fallen, Bush and his chief advisers have made repeated references to Iran, Syria, and other nations considered part of the global threat of terrorism. After new al-Qaeda attacks in Saudi Arabia and Morocco in May 2003, the Bush administration announced that it believed Iran had supported those involved in the attacks and indicated it would make efforts short of war to bring down the Iranian government.

What form those efforts will take is unknown, but the tone of the Bush administration toward these other countries in the immediate aftermath of the victory in Iraq has left many with the impression that it is prepared to use U.S. military force

again. The timing of such operations would likely depend on a number of factors, including world opinion and military readiness to mount another offensive. Even short wars cost billions of dollars and require extraordinary planning and management. This factor, combined with economic problems at home, makes it unlikely that any new military offensives will occur any time soon. However, the military's role has been clearly established as central to the president's vision of the war on terror, not just as battle forces but as policers of a fragile and uneasy peace.

U.S. officers intervene after a wedding party in Baghdad gets out of control.

Chapter Two

The Covert War Against International Terror

When President George W. Bush first outlined the war on terror within days of the September 11 attacks, he predicted that rooting out terrorists would include both "drama visible on TV, and covert operations, secret even in success," and that "many [would] be involved in this effort, from FBI agents, to intelligence operatives."[10] His prediction was borne out by the first death to occur in the war on terror in Afghanistan. In an inmate rebellion at the military prison at Mazar-e Sharif, captive Taliban and al-Qaeda members killed Johnny Micheal Spann, an intelligence officer with the U.S. Central Intelligence Agency (CIA). Spann was there as part of a cooperative effort between that agency and the U.S. military to interrogate prisoners for information leading to more arrests. In the words of *New York Times* reporter James Risen, "The fact that the first American to die in combat in Afghanistan was an intelligence officer and not a uniformed soldier serves to underscore the scope of the [CIA's] role in the war in Afghanistan."[11]

Indeed, CIA officers trained and provided logistical and intelligence support to American armed forces during the war in Afghanistan. Special Forces units known for covert operations, such as the U.S. Navy SEALs (Sea, Air, Land) and the U.S. Army Green Berets, have also played an important role there and in the larger war on terror. Their activities are in some respects similar to the CIA's, including training other nations' antiterrorism forces in covert operations, but focus more on conducting secret missions to track down terrorist leaders and cooperating in joint covert missions with other countries.

The Role of Special Forces

The "visible" wars in Afghanistan and Iraq began with aerial bombardment, but the military campaign had actually started much earlier, when Special Forces soldiers infiltrated those countries to assess the situation there. For example, within days of September 11, a small group of Green Berets, assigned to an effort known as Task Force Dagger, were already operating in Afghanistan. They did groundwork typical of Special Forces officers, including working secretly to acquire information that

CIA officer Mike Spann was the first American casualty of the war in Afghanistan.

31

could be used to assist larger military efforts, such as the location of weapons and the condition of roads. They also carried out missions to destroy terrorist property and arrest or kill individuals before they could mount any further attacks.

Another effort, known as Task Force K-BAR (named after a type of military knife), included SEALs and Green Beret commandos. This force fought "secret battles," according to journalist Mark Mazzetti, "to root out terrorism throughout the country [operating] in a murky world where success is sometimes hard to measure and outright victory even harder to declare." [12]

While hundreds of bombs were dropped in an area known to have been used as a camp by al-Qaeda, the SEALs of Task Force K-BAR set up camp in the nearby town of Khost. There they watched and waited for any information that might allow them to zero in on a terrorist hideout and launch a lightning raid. Additionally, after each bombing run against a cave com-

Members of the U.S. Army's Eighty-Second Airborne place explosives inside a cave containing al-Qaeda weapons.

مُجاهد اِسلام
اُسامہ بن لادن

نُورِ خُدا ہے کفر کی حرکت پہ خندہ زن
پُھونکوں سے یہ چراغ بُجھایا نہ جائے گا

An al-Qaeda recruiting poster depicts Osama bin Laden as the mastermind behind the terrorist attacks of September 11.

plex at Zhawar, they scouted the area for evidence and to hunt down any remaining al-Qaeda operatives. Among the things they found were caches of weapons and expensive communications equipment as well as what Mazzetti describes as "a terrorist classroom decorated with pictures of New York City and tourist landmarks around the world. Al-Qaeda recruiting posters hung on the walls, one depicting a serene Osama bin Laden surrounded by fighter jets and a plane crashing into the World Trade Center."[13]

Special Forces operations like Task Force K-BAR begin when agents slip in under cover of darkness to stake out the chosen target. After this reconnaissance, a decision is made as to the best way to move on the target. In the case of the al-Qaeda complex at Shkin, in eastern Afghanistan, four miles from the Pakistan border, more Special Operations troops and marines were brought in by helicopter. They launched a raid that resulted in thirty arrests and the seizure of caches of weapons and explosives. Another raid at the town of Yaya Kahil was the largest Army Special Forces direct-action mission since the Vietnam War. There, a ninety-minute raid by approximately one hundred soldiers yielded stockpiles of weapons, satellite phones, and computers holding information about al-Qaeda operations, and seven suspects were taken prisoner.

Support of Ground Troops

The success of Special Forces soldiers early in the campaign minimized later ground troop involvement in Afghanistan, resulting in extremely low loss of life among American troops. As author Robin Moore points out, "Most people think it took 5,000 to 40,000 US troops to free Kabul. They are vastly mistaken—fewer than 100 American soldiers were on the ground when Kabul fell." [14]

The approximately four thousand American soldiers arriving in Afghanistan after the fall of the Taliban were used in limited capacities. The first was as a guard or cover force at terrorist camps that had been seized by Afghan fighters and whose occupants had been killed or captured. While Afghans rifled through these bases for evidence of terrorist activities and plans, as well as clues to the whereabouts of terrorist leaders, U.S. Marines stood ready to prevent or counter sneak attacks on the Afghans by those loyal to the Taliban and al-Qaeda. In the Tora Bora campaign, American soldiers also participated in searches of camps and caves whose occupants had fled. The success of these tactics in avoiding casualties was near complete. Only one U.S. soldier was killed in the Tora Bora search of late 2001 and early 2002.

After the Taliban fell, some American troops and Special Forces officers remained, but their numbers are not clear. In

2003, as part of the cooperative arrangement with the Karzai government, sweeps for terrorists and rebels continued to occur, using various combinations of Special Forces and ground troops from both countries. In March 2003, Operation Valiant Strike was undertaken on the Pakistan border, where small numbers of suspected Taliban and al-Qaeda operatives had been attacking Afghan government posts. Several were arrested in Operation Valiant Strike, and a number of munitions caches were discovered, including rocket-propelled grenades,

U.S. Special Forces troops (left) and Afghan men shake hands after the liberation of Mazar-e Sharif from the Taliban.

land mines, and mortar rounds, evidence that terrorism is still a threat in Afghanistan.

The Role of the CIA

The Special Operations Group (SOG) of the Central Intelligence Agency also provides undercover support to military operations in the war on terror. The SOG is a civilian agency but shares many of the same goals and activities as the military Special Forces, although on a much smaller scale. (A total of approximately forty-four thousand officers serve in

A U.S. Navy SEAL carefully inspects a subterranean al-Qaeda prison cell.

the Special Forces units of the armed forces, compared with only several hundred in the SOG.) Special Forces and SOG operatives are similarly trained in guerrilla warfare, infiltration of hostile nations, and covert communication.

Because they play such similar roles in the field, considerable friction has arisen between the CIA and the military over defining the limits of their respective activities. Military officials argue that the CIA should limit itself to collecting and supplying intelligence for the marines, navy, and other branches to use. The CIA disagrees, claiming that working outside of the military bureaucracy gives SOG operatives more flexibility and creativity in the field, and enables them to react more quickly and independently. As a result, the CIA argues, the SOG is in the best possible position to undertake covert operations to track down terrorists.

However, the CIA was not founded for the purpose of undertaking secret missions. The Central Intelligence Agency was established after World War II to ensure that events such as the Japanese surprise attack on Pearl Harbor did not happen again, in the belief that an adequate spy and intelligence network would have uncovered and thwarted the Japanese plans. Thus, the CIA's major responsibility became overseas intelligence gathering, to complement the FBI's efforts inside the United States. With the establishment of SOG, journalist Douglas Waller reports, the CIA moved "beyond the realm of collecting secrets to intervening forcibly in the affairs of foreign states." [15]

However, the CIA's record was embarrassingly poor and often morally troubling, including botched assassination attempts on foreign leaders Patrice Lumumba of the Congo and Fidel Castro of Cuba, and support of coups to overthrow governments the United States opposed. As a result, the SOG's role, and the CIA's budget for covert operations, had been greatly curtailed in recent years in the belief, summarized by Waller, that "billion dollar spy satellites collected intelligence more efficiently [than the CIA] and without embarrassing the US." [16]

President Bush announces that the FBI and CIA will cooperate to fight terrorism. The CIA gathers intelligence overseas, while the FBI works in the United States.

A Revitalized SOG

That was all to change after September 11. Many analysts felt al-Qaeda had succeeded in its coordinated, devastating attacks because of a lack of intelligence of the sort that can only be provided by well-trained and highly skilled covert operatives working undercover inside terrorist groups. Addressing this lack, the CIA began increasing the number of undercover agents and their extent of operations around the world. The SOG has, as a result, become one of the CIA's main contributions to the war on terror. Today several hundred SOG officers are in place in Central Asia, North Africa, East Asia, and Pakistan. SOG speedboats can put operatives on shore and small SOG jets can fly agents anywhere in the world on only a few hours' notice. SOG cargo planes and ships deliver agents and equipment wherever they are needed. This investment in human operatives has come about as a result of what Waller calls a clearer understanding that "technology has its limitations. Satellites, for instance, can't see inside buildings [and] phone taps can't capture an enemy's every move."[17]

The new emphasis is once again on the individual agent working undercover to develop intelligence. "Name a country anywhere, and [the CIA] can identify with a few phone calls four or five people who will have a variety of skills to go into that country.... We have the ability to hide in plain sight, get in and get out before anybody figures out who we are,"[18] an unnamed CIA source recently told *Time* magazine. Using such tactics, CIA agents have played a central role in apprehending al-Qaeda members in a number of successful operations all over the globe, often in cooperation with police and intelligence agencies of the countries where the terrorists were hiding.

"America's Cops Overseas"

One additional arm of the government involved in covert activities in the war on terror is the Diplomatic Security Service, or DSS, a branch of the Department of State. The twelve hundred

Members of the U.S. Diplomatic Security Service guard the site of a meeting of Iraqi opposition leaders in Baghdad.

agents of the DSS are both Foreign Service professionals and sworn law enforcement officers, responsible for the security of diplomatic staff overseas. Since its founding in 1985, DSS agents have been "America's cops overseas," according to international law enforcement expert Samuel Katz, who refers to them as having "badges without borders." [19] Their job is to protect embassy staff, serve as bodyguards to diplomats, and advise ambassadors on matters of security.

In recent years, however, the job of a DSS agent has increasingly involved terrorist tracking and apprehension because many acts of terrorism since the 1990s have been attacks on embassies. On August 7, 1998, for example, car bombs exploded at the American embassies in Nairobi, Kenya, and Dar es Salaam, Tanzania, killing 224 people. A radical Islamic group linked to Osama bin Laden claimed responsibility for the attacks. One day later the DSS established a website link that collected hundreds of tips as part of the State Department's multimillion-dollar rewards program for information leading to terrorist arrest.

The DSS has also been credited with playing a role in tracking down an Iraqi connection to a failed attempt to bomb the U.S. embassy in Manila and in the search for terrorist mastermind Ramzi Yousef, who is accused of planning the World Trade Center bombing in 1993. Though its activities are often overshadowed by FBI and CIA operations, the DSS continues to play a direct role in the war on terror.

Chapter Three

The Technological War on Terror

U se of military troops and covert operations are two major components in the war on terror, but state-of-the-art high technology is also an integral part of missions that hunt down terrorists. Technology provides essential information the CIA and Special Forces need, and new weapons and surveillance techniques have in some situations taken the place of field operatives in the war on terror. Technology is preferred in some situations for a particular key advantage: It can often be employed without putting anyone in physical danger.

The military makes substantial use of modern technology in nearly all its missions. Often several different kinds of technology are used in concert. For example, the presence of a wanted terrorist may be initially detected electronically through such means as cellular or satellite airwaves. Then a more conventional weapon such as a bomb or guided missile may be dropped on that location. In modern warfare, the majority of bombs and missiles fall into the category of what are nicknamed "smart bombs." This refers to explosives that are precisely guided by sensors or remote control devices to a target. Smart bombs, for example, were used at the outset of the war on Iraq when intelligence sources believed they had pinpointed Saddam Hussein's exact location. Unmanned aircraft known as predator drones can find and destroy even a very small moving target. In Yemen in November 2002, five

Members of the Eleventh Reconnaissance Squadron examine an unmanned predator drone before a mission.

al-Qaeda operatives, including one American, were killed in their car by such a strike by the CIA.

These very precise weapons are at the highly visible forefront of modern warfare, but they are really only a small part of technological advances already in place to fight terror or currently under development. Much of the new technology cannot be used as weapons in the conventional sense of physically injuring an enemy; rather, these sophisticated tools expose the enemy and his sources of support, a huge advantage in waging war. Such technological advances not only assist the United States in tracking down terrorists but enable it to provide specific information to foreign countries so they can win the war on terror within their own borders.

Eavesdropping on Terrorists

Telephones, cell phones, and e-mail enable everyone to communicate better, including terrorists, but advanced communication systems have also benefited those who track terrorists down. Sophisticated phone surveillance, for example, is becoming an effective means of locating terrorists. The National Security Agency (NSA), the largest U.S. intelligence agency, is responsible for intercepting and analyzing massive amounts of foreign voice, video, and other communication as well as protecting U.S. government communications. One new software program breaks down speech into phonemes, the units of sound that make up words, and recognizes specific words with 98 percent accuracy, regardless of the speaker's dialect or accent. Its computational speed is amazing; it can search twenty hours of audio recording in less than one second and identify certain words, names, and secret codes likely to be associated with terrorist activity. This software can be loaded on laptops

U.S. Special Forces survey the front line of northern Iraq using highly advanced observational equipment.

and used in the field as part of wiretapping and bugging activities.

Terrorists risk exposing themselves through many other forms of communication because of new technologies' ability to intercept messages. For example, before the hunt for bin Laden intensified in the wake of September 11, he was known to use satellite phones. Because it is now quite possible to locate a person by intercepting a satellite call, he has since abandoned this method of communication. Direct communications by e-mail are also very risky because of a number of programs that are used to hone in on and read electronic messages.

More common is terrorists' use of websites to post information, using hidden codes or other markers. According to a

A Taliban leader uses a satellite phone to confirm the identity of a journalist. U.S. forces eavesdrop on such phone calls as a means of identifying terrorists.

July 2002 CNN report, "Al-Qaeda is said to be computer savvy, and some investigators believe they have found markers or code words that indicate bin Laden is trying to signal supporters he is alive."[20] Captured al-Qaeda members have revealed that their organization uses sophisticated technology known as steganography to hide messages inside photographic files on completely unrelated types of websites, including pornographic sites. The photographs are the equivalent of throwing a blanket over something one wishes to hide, making it difficult for the various detection programs to get beyond the photograph to read the encrypted data. Site addresses are changed frequently to minimize the chance of being caught, and the enormity of the Internet makes hidden messages an effective, although complicated, way of communicating.

James Bamford, a prominent expert on national security, says that al-Qaeda's means of communication are "a combination of low-tech communication with supporters, communicating by messaging or couriers, and using the Internet to reach others."[21] In other words, al-Qaeda and other groups use whatever seems to be the most effective and least risky means of communication at the moment, from hopping on airplanes to deliver messages in person to carefully and laboriously embedding a message on the Internet. Journalist Daniel Sieberg agrees that "within the veiled and shadowy network of Osama bin Laden's operation, information is likely communicated through both high- and low-tech means, using everything from a web page to a whisper."[22]

In part, the continued need to communicate face-to-face is due to improvements in counterterrorist technologies. An example of one such breakthrough is the FBI's state-of-the-art computer program known as Carnivore, which is capable of detecting even the most cleverly encrypted messages. Also in this class is the top-secret Echelon system, a satellite-based network that monitors a wide range of worldwide communications, making it harder to communicate.

Even with such advanced technologies, however, it is difficult to stay ahead of online terrorist activity. General Mike

Hayden, the director of the NSA, commented after September 11 that "we are behind the curve in keeping up with the global technological revolution,"[23] and Bruce Schneier, an expert in cryptology, the art of making and breaking codes, adds that "the years of the military being at the leading edge of technology are gone because it moves so fast. In the real world . . . everyone has access to the same stuff. The limitations are basically just money."[24] Regrettably, money is a commodity bin Laden and al-Qaeda do not lack.

Faces in a Crowd

Eavesdropping is only one technological means to zero in on terrorists. Research aimed at identifying individuals by various methods of facial scanning began in the 1980s at the Massachusetts Institute of Technology Media Lab, and use of the technology has grown recently in the hope that it will be helpful in the war on terror. Face recognition, or faceprinting, as this technology is sometimes called, is part of the new "biometrics" industry, which is based on analyzing precise measurements of many parts of the face, such as the bridge of the nose, the corner of the mouth, and the cheekbone. The underlying theory is that no two individuals have exactly the same measurement profile, just as no two have exactly the same fingerprints. Today the two leading companies in this field are Identix and Viisage. Identix software takes up to 80 different measurements of the distance between specific parts of the face to identify an individual. Viisage software takes a different approach, creating 128 images of the face from different aspects and angles, called eigenfaces, to build a multidimensional picture called a face space. Both systems then store those visual images in a database, with which images of unknown individuals can be compared.

Face recognition systems are intended to be used at entrances to prominent buildings or other public places that might be targets for terrorist acts. Specially placed cameras will scan a crowd and send the data to an Identix or Viisage database. As people go by, their faces would be "read" and matches with known terrorists could be made. One particularly promising use of such technology is for screening in airports. Trials of various faceprint programs are in place in a few locations around the world, including the airport in Reykjavik, Iceland, a major stopover point for the long transatlantic flights terrorists often must take.

However, even when the conditions are most favorable, when a very clear photo of an individual looking directly into the camera is fed into a database, the technology is not yet reliable. A recent trial of Identix at the airport in Palm Beach, Florida, was a disappointment, as fifteen employees who had volunteered to be identified in the database as terrorists were spotted only 47 percent of the time. Conversely, a passenger was falsely identified as a terrorist by the system at a rate of

Computer programs that faceprint individuals offer tremendous potential to identify terrorists at airports.

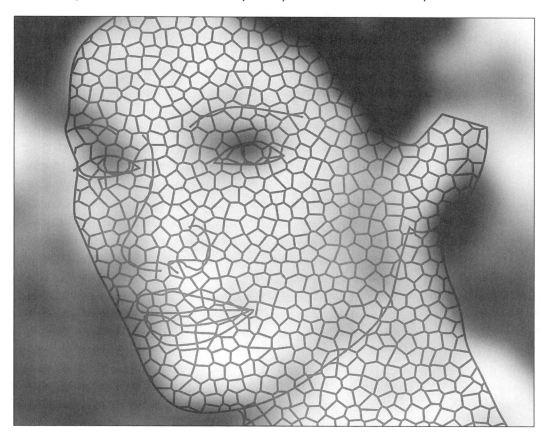

once every half-hour. It appears that such face recognition software programs are still far from being able to pick out individuals accurately enough to be useful in the war on terror.

Identifying terrorists by faceprinting will not be made easier simply by improving the system. Terrorists protect their identities very carefully, and photographs, if they exist at all, tend to be of very poor quality. A grainy photograph of a person looking to the side with his or her face partly in shadow is not likely to provide sufficient data to create a database profile. The chances of identifying a person by using this technology are also reduced if the person does not look directly into the camera. Researchers disagree about the extent to which disguises, changes in health, or the aging process can affect face recognition. Plastic surgery also further complicates the issue of recognition of an individual.

Other technologies such as fingerprint databases and eyeprints, which scan the coloration patterns of the iris, have similar drawbacks because terrorists' eyeprints are not likely to be on file already, nor are their fingerprints, unless they have been previously arrested. Even if such files exist, it is unlikely that a terrorist would willingly cooperate in providing the on-the-spot match. For practical reasons, therefore, in addition to technological problems, there are no immediate plans to implement such procedures as eyeprinting passengers before they board planes. Likewise, scenarios in which cameras scan a crowd at the Super Bowl or a World Cup match and identify one face among thousands just before he carries out an act of mass destruction are likely to remain more the stuff of movies than reality for some time to come. Nevertheless, considerable effort is going into developing reliable identification systems, which would be a major tool for tracking down terrorists if their accuracy can be improved.

Ubicomp and Data-Mining

Technologies such as faceprinting are part of what is now being described by the buzzword *ubicomp*, which stands for "ubiq-

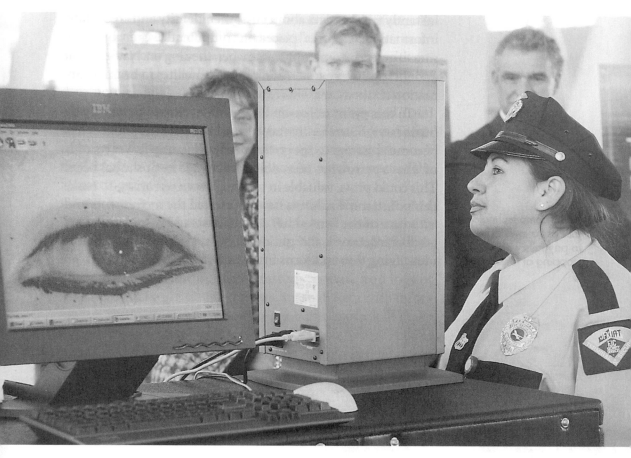

uitous computing." Ubicomp refers to technology that is all-seeing, or everywhere at once. The central goal of ubicomp is to develop new ways of tracking things and people. Speaking to its extreme pervasiveness and potential to infiltrate daily life, ubicomp is described by journalist Elizabeth Weise as "a gentle dusting of almost microscopic sensors in everything we use, wear, walk on and drive, all calling out to each other in a radio whisper we never hear or see, but that tracks us like a mother following a two year old child."[25] Already some ubicomp has entered daily life. Electronic ATM and credit card transactions enable people to purchase items without using cash. Transponders like EZ Pass allow people to travel on pay roads without stopping at toll booths. Technologies communicate

A security agent tests an iris-scanning device that will be used to identify airport employees.

Defense for the ultimate purpose of catching individuals engaging in illegal activities. Though many might argue that a person who is doing nothing wrong has nothing to fear, concern is growing that creating detailed databanks on even the most law-abiding of citizens is an unconstitutional invasion of privacy because it arbitrarily includes people there is no reason to suspect of anything.

TIA is at this stage only a controversial proposal by the Bush administration, not an implemented program. Its progress has been slowed by the vigorous objections of many legislators and powerful groups representing a wide spectrum of liberal and conservative viewpoints. Susan Graham, a Republican senator from Maine and head of the Senate Governmental Affairs Committee, says that it "raises extraordinary concerns about individual privacy." [27] Former House majority leader Dick Armey, a Republican from Texas, called TIA "the only thing that is scary to me." [28] Coming from members of Bush's own party, these objections are an indication of strong feeling that TIA violates basic privacy rights. To date, TIA has been stalled by congressional refusal to allocate funds for it, but the Bush administration has not abandoned the idea.

Terrorists move all too easily in a free society, and few would deny that it is important to use the vast powers of computers to aid in tracking down and apprehending individuals intent on violence. How this can be done without undercutting the public's rights to live without undue government interference will be one of the great challenges of the continuing war on terror.

Chapter Four

Winning Global Support to Fight Terror

Occasionally news headlines trumpet the capture of a high-profile terrorist, such as the arrest in Pakistan in March 2003 of Khalid Shaikh Mohammad, the al-Qaeda leader said to be the mastermind of the events of September 11. Despite the significance of such arrests, the news stories are often strikingly undramatic. Observers often describe an unassuming resident of a quiet neighborhood being arrested while he slept, or ate, or visited friends. There were no bombs, just an uneventful stakeout followed by a quick raid. The arrest of Khalid Shaikh Mohammad followed this pattern. At 2:30 A.M. a house was raided, based on a tip from neighbors hoping for a reward who had noticed a stranger in their neighborhood. Unknown to them, this stranger was the third highest ranking member of al-Qaeda. Acting on this tip, Pakistani police moved in, and quickly and without bloodshed arrested Mohammad and a companion.

What appeared on the surface to be simple and ordinary was in fact the result of delicate and complex cooperation between the governments of Pakistan and the United States. Such diplomacy is required in the war on terror. President Bush said as much, in his first major address to Congress and the American public after September 11: "We ask every nation to join us. We will ask, and we will need, the help of police forces, intelligence services, and banking systems around the world."[29] What this has meant in practice is that behind every terrorist arrest in a foreign country is a story of collaboration with foreign officials, ranging from heads of government to local police chiefs.

These negotiations are designed to help the United States capture wanted terrorists while respecting the sovereignty of other nations. As the richest and most powerful nation in the world, what the United States offers in return for cooperation is whatever financial, political, military, or other support is most needed by the government of the foreign country involved. However, concerns often arise in the international community about how the United States uses its extraordinary power, and the enormous pressure it can exert on weaker nations. Mixed reactions to U.S. requests for cooperation have resulted in a great deal of international tension as the war on terror progresses.

Using Economic Clout

Some nations such as Great Britain work effectively with the United States because they generally agree with American objectives and share American values. Others cooperate because they need the wealth the United States can offer. The United States provides billions of dollars in foreign aid each year. Offers of more aid are a key way the United States persuades reluctant nations to support its goals. In addition to direct monetary assistance, future economic development is often offered in the form of promises to help build highways, airports, dams, factories, and other costly infrastructure that strengthens countries by enabling them to become more competitive and more self-sufficient. Other economic incentives include granting what is known as favored nation trading status, which allows for certain tariff reductions that benefit the foreign country.

A prominent example of how economic pressure can result in cooperation by otherwise reluctant or unfriendly nations occurred in Pakistan. Before the September 11 attacks, Pakistan was one of only three countries in the world (along with the United Arab Emirates and Saudi Arabia) recognizing the

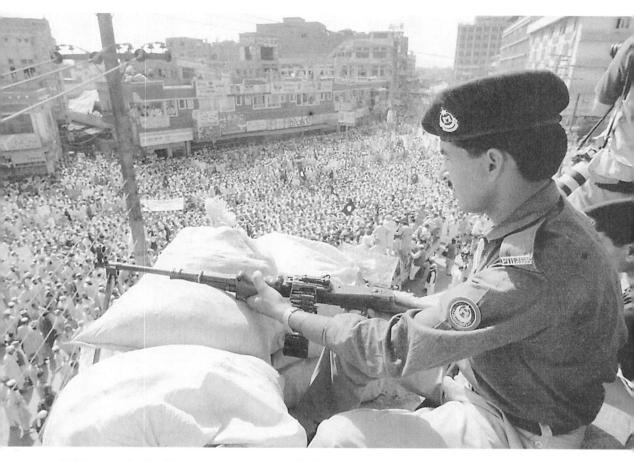

Taliban as the legitimate government of Afghanistan. Pakistan had not traditionally been considered an ally of the United States. In fact, it had been subject to American economic sanctions as a result of its acquisition and testing of nuclear weapons as part of its ongoing conflict with neighboring India, a long-standing U.S. ally.

In the immediate aftermath of September 11, however, Pakistan's president, Pervez Musharraf, was faced with a difficult choice. The Bush administration made it clear that it expected Pakistan's cooperation in tracking down Taliban and al-Qaeda members who had crossed the border from Afghanistan into Pakistan. Musharraf was concerned that a refusal might result in stronger U.S. support for India in the

A Pakistani police officer monitors an anti-American protest near a local mosque.

struggle over the resource-rich Kashmir province on the India-Pakistan border. He also worried that a refusal would make Pakistan look like a supporter of terror in the eyes of the world. On the other hand, Musharraf was well aware of Pakistan's strong and vocal core of radical Muslims, who openly threatened a backlash against Musharraf if he cooperated with the United States in hunting down fellow Muslims.

Musharraf was willing to risk this backlash because what the United States offered was too significant to turn down. Pakistan was staggering economically under a $35 billion loan debt from other countries and international agencies. Its

Pakistani radical Muslims riot during a protest against U.S. involvement in Afghanistan.

domestic debt was equally devastating. The Bush administration offered an aid package worth over a billion dollars and agreed to forgive an additional billion dollars in debt, and to reduce trade barriers and other economic sanctions against Pakistan so it could make money on its exports.

Similar aid packages have been offered to other countries, not always with equal success. For example, Turkey refused to allow the United States to station sixty-two thousand troops on Turkish soil, which foiled U.S. plans to launch an invasion of Iraq from the north. The United States had offered Turkey an aid package including $6 billion in grants for Turkish cooperation, but the Turks strongly opposed the U.S. action in Iraq and could not reach an agreement.

Threatening the Uncooperative

In some cases, especially among smaller, developing countries, threats of boycotts, trade embargoes, reducing direct aid, and other sanctions are used to convince a country to go along with American requests. Countries may be more likely to bow to economic pressure, however, simply because the alternative might be submitting to military force.

The United States has by far the most powerful military in the world, and American leaders have proven their willingness to use military force when economic sanctions fail. This was the case in Iraq, after President Saddam Hussein repeatedly fell short of both UN and U.S. demands to disclose his inventory of weapons and dispose of weapons he was forbidden by the United Nations to have.

After declaring an end to diplomacy and negotiations, it took the United States only a few weeks to cross over from Kuwait, traverse Iraq, enter Baghdad, and topple Saddam's regime. Subsequently, key administration figures such as Secretary of State Colin Powell and Secretary of Defense Donald Rumsfeld visited the region, and in their speeches and meetings hinted at the possibility that the military would be used again if countries such as Syria and Iran did not take a stronger stand in rejecting terrorists and their methods. The Bush administration has clearly signaled its intention to keep the pressure on all countries it considers important to the war on terror, using both the carrot and the stick.

Cooperative Policing

In the case of Pakistan, even with the powerful package of incentives offered by the United States, Musharraf knew that his alliance with the United States would be hard to sell to his people, many of whom harbor strong anti-American sentiment. He agreed to cooperate by allowing only a very limited military presence in Pakistan. Though American forces have been permitted to chase suspected terrorists across the border from Afghanistan into Pakistan if they are in "hot pursuit," and to assist in covert operations, Pakistan expects U.S. forces to stay on the Afghan side of the border. Their role is to provide technical support and advice to Pakistani law enforcement and generally to go no further than that. Pakistan's Inter-Services Intelligence Agency (ISI) is ultimately responsible for conducting intelligence gathering and stakeouts and making arrests. Typically, American operatives are present when arrests are made and during interrogations, but both countries take great pains to stress the Pakistani role. The important point is that the United States is not violating Pakistan's sovereign right to handle all aspects of law enforcement and military action in its own country.

Thus, cooperative policing has become one of the major components of the war on terror. The capture in early 2003 of Khalid Shaikh Mohammad was a prime example, as was the arrest of Abu Zubadayah, a top al-Qaeda leader, in March 2002. Zubadayah escaped Afghanistan in September 2001 and went into hiding in Pakistan. His whereabouts came to light after two men disguised as Afghan women were caught at a border checkpoint by Pakistani police. Under interrogation, the men revealed knowledge of Zubadayah's presence in Faisalabad, Pakistan. Communication detection devices were then used to pinpoint his location, and Pakistani authorities called in the Faisalabad police to close in.

Police clipped electric wires and snuck into the target house around 3:00 A.M., where they surprised and subdued guards. Zubadayah and others ran to the roof and jumped to a neighboring rooftop, where more Pakistani police were waiting. In the melee that ensued, Zubadayah and a companion were shot and another accomplice was killed. Two dozen others were arrested in the house. Once the arrests were made, American operatives moved in to identify the suspects and search the hideout, where they found computer disks, notebooks, and

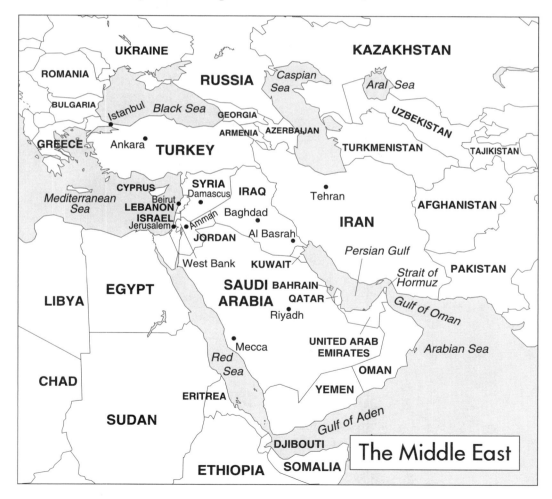

The Middle East

U.S. soldiers search buildings near the Pakistani border for al-Qaeda suspects.

phone numbers—in all, about ten thousand pages of material. This evidence was sent back to the United States for analysis, while the suspects were taken to American bases for questioning. In that month alone in Pakistan, more than sixty al-Qaeda suspects were apprehended in similar cooperative policing efforts.

Equipment and Training

Because the details of covert operations generally remain secret even when a major arrest is made, it is impossible to know the full extent of the American role in covert activities in Pakistan and elsewhere. However, the extent of U.S. technical support, essential to the success of the effort, is more open and obvious. Pakistan's border security has been boosted by the provision of all-terrain vehicles, Apache helicopters, and radio communication equipment. Afghanistan has been similarly equipped, and the United States has spearheaded the training of Afghan and Pakistani police and army officers in use of this equipment and tactics in the war on terror. The ways in which U.S. training has enabled other countries to fight terrorism can be seen perhaps most clearly in the Philippines.

The Philippines were once an American protectorate, and a huge American military presence continued even after Philippine independence in 1948. Although small groups, primarily Filipino Muslims, have been consistently hostile to the

U.S. soldiers wait for a helicopter during a covert operation near the Pakistani border.

United States, for the most part relationships between the two countries have been cordial. In recent years, the Philippines have been troubled by several terrorist groups, most notably Abu Sayyaf ("Bearer of the Sword"), whose goal is similar to that of other groups in neighboring countries—to establish an independent fundamentalist Islamic state in Southeast Asia.

Speaking for the Bush administration, Secretary of Defense Donald Rumsfeld has stated that "if we have to go into 15 more countries, we ought to do it to fight terrorism." [30] The president of the Philippines, Gloria Macapagal Arroyo, saw in this message an opportunity to get American assistance in fighting Abu Sayyaf. Though Filipino law forbids allowing foreigners to fight on Philippine soil, an exception provides for visiting forces joining in noncombat military exercises. Arroyo worked with the United States to create a joint military exercise designed to train Filipino soldiers to track down Abu Sayyaf members and other terrorists. In January 2002, 650 American soldiers,

Police escort Karim Kiram Hassan (center), a member of Abu Sayyaf, after a raid in the Philippines.

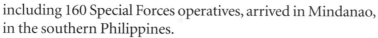

including 160 Special Forces operatives, arrived in Mindanao, in the southern Philippines.

The purpose of these exercises was primarily to train Filipino soldiers to use new technologies that would help them combat terrorism in their own country. The American military training was judged a success, especially because the leader of Abu Sayyaf was killed during the joint operation, in a dramatic skirmish that took place on a small boat off the coast of the Philippines. The new skills the Philippine army had acquired were a major factor in their ability to carry out this mission. In January 2003 a new group of U.S. soldiers and advisers arrived to take part in another round of training including advanced night flying skills. It appears that the Philippines might serve as an example of how the United States can work with other countries to fight terror in ways which respect their leadership and national sovereignty.

Some question the long-term advisability of this broad technical support, however. Neither Pakistan nor Afghanistan has a long history of alliance with the United States, and indeed it is uncertain whether the friendship will outlast the current president of either country. If Muslim extremists are able to gain more power in Pakistan or Afghanistan, all the equipment and training offered by the United States could potentially be used against it. International relations in this part of the world are complex and go beyond the war on terror. For example, there is concern that U.S. help in strengthening the Pakistani armed forces may lead to escalating tension between Pakistan and India, its long-standing enemy. Alliances built on such whims threaten important partnerships in the region, such as that between the United States and India, and must be undertaken with great care and sensitivity.

With or Without Global Support?

America's relations and sometimes fragile alliances with many other countries around the world were unquestionably harmed by the stance taken by the United States against Iraq. To many nations, Iraq was not a threat to the region or the world because its army and its weapons had been greatly reduced in a long war against Iran as well as the first Gulf War in 1991. Instead of going to war, many nations favored giving UN weapons inspectors more time to comb Iraq, arguing that this was the safest and most humanitarian way to determine what Iraq did and did not have in its arsenal.

How to Reduce Terrorism?

The position of the United States and its sole significant ally, Great Britain, was that Saddam Hussein had to be removed from power so that a serious and imminent threat could be removed from the world. Although the Bush administration claimed there was a strong possibility that Saddam would supply al-Qaeda with weapons, links between al-Qaeda and the Iraqi regime have not been documented. The war on terror is very different from other wars, and its goals are rather imprecise. As a result, many Americans supported the war simply to see a ruthless dictator stripped of power, and because invading and conquering was a familiar and easily understandable way to confront an enemy. Whether it was actually fought over terrorism and whether it has actually reduced terrorism remains to be seen.

How to reduce terrorism is indeed a major worldwide concern that many nations feel the Bush administration has not adequately addressed. When Bush announced the war on terror shortly after September 11, he categorized the nations of the world as either supporters of the United States or supporters of terrorists. At the time, concerns about his possible oversimplification of the problem took a backseat to the legitimate need to bring al-Qaeda and other terrorist groups under control. Since 2001, however, defining a country as "friend" or "enemy" on the basis of one issue—terrorism—has been called into question. A case in point is Pakistan, whose new status as an ally is troubling to many who see more threat than friendship brewing there. Saudi Arabia has been considered an

American ally for decades, but most of the September 11 hijackers came from that country and the invasion of Iraq prompted reexamination of that alliance despite Saudi support in other areas. Countries such as France and Germany, who led the opposition to the war in Iraq, have long-standing good relationships with the United States but have been alienated by the Bush administration's policies and actions. Few, however, would seriously consider France and Germany enemies of the United States.

As the war on terror took center stage in American foreign policy, and the Bush administration began to focus on a war with Iraq, many countries perceived America as a bully whose actions were undermining long-standing, hard-won, and valuable international bonds that preserved peace. The Bush administration, on the other hand, believed that the United Nations and other world bodies lacked the initiative and will to go beyond endless and ultimately fruitless diplomatic negotiation and that only force would make real headway in the war on terror.

Whatever merit there may be in these differing positions, it is clear that relationships between the United States and most nations around the world, including some of its staunchest allies, have been significantly affected by Bush's decision to go to war in Iraq without UN support. Some fear that efforts to defeat al-Qaeda and other terrorists will dissolve as resources and media attention are focused on Iraq. Others contend that the war in Iraq is likely to create a new generation of people with a grudge against the United States and thus undermine the chances for winning the war on terror. It remains to be seen what steps must be taken to ensure the kind of global support the United States needs to wage the war on terror.

Chapter Five

International Terrorists in Custody

Tracking terrorists and making arrests is one aspect of the overall global war on terror, but an equally important and equally complex aspect is the handling of suspected terrorists once they have been apprehended. The first issue is the processing and imprisonment of terrorists. The second involves getting them to reveal information about other terrorists and their plans. Like much about this new kind of war, the treatment of terrorists in custody involves new strategies and methods and has yielded mixed results.

Processing Arrestees

Those arrested for terrorism generally fall into one of two categories. The first is terrorist leaders such as Khalid Shaikh Mohammad. When such important people are captured, where they are kept and how they are being treated is kept secret. For example, after his arrest in Pakistan, Khalid Shaikh Mohammad was quickly whisked away for questioning by U.S. authorities, and he will most likely be held in solitary confinement in an undisclosed location until he is brought to trial in the United States.

The second, much larger category of arrestees includes those caught in sweeps, such as occurred in Afghanistan at the time of the fall of the Taliban. Lower-level operatives and substantial numbers of detainees who have been captured or who have surrendered in groups are usually taken as a group to a secure facility operated by the arresting country or a nearby American military base, such as the one at Bagram, Afghanistan. There they are questioned to determine their citizenship and, to the degree possible, their connection to terrorist activity. In some cases it is immediately apparent that a person has no terrorist connections and has simply been in the wrong place at the wrong time; such individuals are released. This is a fairly unusual occurrence, however, because it is often difficult to sort

A Northern Alliance official interrogates a captured Taliban prisoner in Afghanistan.

through the stories of each detainee and determine with confidence whose claims of noninvolvement are true. As a result, many detainees have been in custody for several years.

Guantánamo Bay

Once American military action in Afghanistan began, individuals in custody quickly numbered in the hundreds. A facil-

U.S. Marines escort a detainee at Camp X-Ray in Guantánamo Bay, Cuba.

ity known as Camp X-Ray, originally erected at the U.S. military base at Guantánamo Bay in Cuba to house Haitian refugees in the 1990s, was quickly converted into a makeshift prison for Taliban, al-Qaeda, and other arrestees who were moved there from Afghanistan in early 2002.

The original detainees in Camp X-Ray numbered around one hundred primarily Muslim men. They were housed in six-by-eight-foot enclosures, consisting of chain-link fencing for walls, tin roofs, and concrete floors. They were given thin mats and blankets for use in sleep and to kneel on for daily prayer. Photographs of the prisoners in what amounted to cages, kneeling with their hands tied behind their backs, some wearing goggles, earmuffs, and other devices designed to keep them from seeing and hearing, created an uproar among human rights groups around the world. Later, inmates' diets were adjusted to conform to Muslim religious laws, and they were given Qur'ans, the holy book of Islam. Medical care improved, and they were permitted to regrow their characteristic beards, which had been shaved upon their arrest.

The U.S. government also responded to widespread concerns voiced by the Red Cross and other groups by constructing a more permanent facility in Guantánamo Bay called Camp Delta. At this site, large crates used for international shipping were divided into 5.5-by-8-foot cells, with steel mesh replacing three sides of the original container. Half the cell space is taken up by a metal bed that is welded to the one solid wall, and there is barely room to stand and stretch. According to reporter Richard Phillips, "These cells are smaller than the death row facilities in Texas, where inmates are allowed to shower and to exercise for an hour outside the cells each day." In contrast, Camp Delta prisoners "are confined to their non–air conditioned cells in fierce tropical heat for all but thirty minutes a week,"[31] when they are allowed to exercise, wearing handcuffs, in a slightly larger 25-by-18-foot enclosure. Not all of those arrested in Afghanistan and neighboring countries are sent to

Afghan men released from Camp X-Ray discuss their prison experiences with journalists.

Guantánamo Bay. North of Kabul, the capital of Afghanistan, a military base at Bagram is being used by the United States as a detention center. Typical conditions there are similar to those at Guantánamo Bay.

A Deteriorating Situation

By the middle of 2002 the number of detainees at Guantánamo Bay had grown to over 500, and by mid-2003 the number stood at 650, from forty-three different countries. By the first anniversary of the arrival of the initial group on January 15, 2002, only 5 had been released. By March 2003, 16 Guantánamo detainees had attempted suicide, usually by hanging or suffocation, and 4 of these had tried twice. None succeeded, although one was left in a coma from which it is unlikely he will awaken. One inmate recently pleaded in a letter, "set me free as I am innocent or take me to the court for trial [or let me] die as I cannot stand life in this place."[32] In response to the suicide attempts, U.S. military officials opened a new psychiatric ward at Guantánamo Bay. Though some cells in this ward will be larger, many prisoners will live in similar conditions to those in which they attempted suicide. Some even will remain shackled while they receive psychological counseling and psychiatric care.

Recently several dozen prisoners were moved to a new medium security wing of Camp Delta. There they sleep in a communal dorm and have greater ability to move around. They are allowed to exercise daily and eat and pray together. As many as two hundred may eventually be housed under such conditions—a precursor, American officials say, to their ultimate release and return home either to face trial or regain their liberty. In mid-2003 the Department of Defense, on the heels of revelations that several detainees were young teenagers, announced that a few unidentified prisoners were scheduled

The U.S. government constructed Camp Delta (pictured) in response to concerns over the treatment of Camp X-Ray detainees.

for imminent release and that the government would be moving faster in the future to investigate each prisoner's case. In May 2003 several dozen prisoners left Guantánamo Bay for Afghanistan, but whether they are now free is not clear.

Stress and Duress

Recent investigative reports in newspapers such as the *Washington Post* and the *Wall Street Journal* focus attention not on the conditions at Guantánamo Bay but on allegations of serious mistreatment of prisoners at Bagram, the military detention center in Afghanistan. Autopsies on two prisoners who died there in December 2002 revealed blunt force injuries to their bodies that contributed to their death; both deaths were subsequently ruled homicides.

"Stress and duress" is the name military officers use for the techniques designed to gain information from some terror suspects at Bagram and elsewhere. Stress and duress is not as extreme as deliberate, directly inflicted torture, but its intention—to break prisoners' wills and induce them to reveal information—is the same. A practice called "softening up" of new captives includes beatings by military police and U.S. Army Special Forces. According to *Washington Post* reporters Dana Priest and Barton Gellman, prisoners are "commonly blindfolded and thrown into walls, bound in painful positions, subjected to loud noises and deprived of sleep,"[33] and kept awake by kicks and nonstop bombardment with bright light. They may be forced to stay in one position for hours, and some released detainees have reported that prisoners are chained to the ceiling for extended periods of time and are denied food and drink. Pain medication has been withheld from wounded prisoners to give them further incentive to talk.

Though no one is accusing the United States of the extreme methods of torture used by some repressive regimes around the world, a number of concerns have arisen about practices by which, in the words of reporters Priest and Gellman, "the traditional lines between right and wrong, legal and inhumane, are evolving and blurred."[34] Some Americans argue that it is vital to learn whatever information al-Qaeda suspects have, as

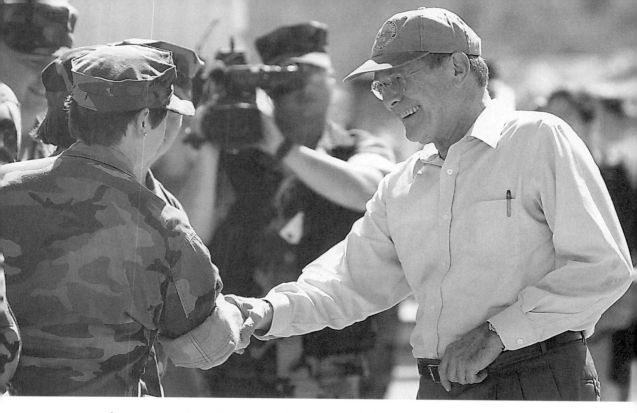

U.S. secretary of defense Donald Rumsfeld greets American troops after a tour of Camp X-Ray. Rumsfeld denies all allegations of prisoner mistreatment.

a way of protecting Americans from future attacks, but many others are deeply troubled by this attitude. In 1999 in a report to the UN Committee Against Torture, the U.S. delegates said, "Americans find torture abhorrent to their very notion of themselves as Americans. The right to be free of torture is an indelible element of the American experience." [35] The same standards apply to American citizens and noncitizens everywhere the U.S. government operates in the world. This basic American value, nevertheless, has been challenged by the war on terror.

Donald Rumsfeld, secretary of defense in the Bush administration, has repeatedly denied that anyone is being tortured at American hands, as defined by the UN Convention on Torture, which the United States ratified in 1994. In that document, torture is defined as "any act by which severe pain or suffering, whether physical or mental, is intentionally inflicted on a person for such purposes as obtaining from him or a third person information or a confession" [36] by a person acting in an official capacity. The Geneva Convention, the most important documents outlining the rights of wartime prisoners, define torture similarly, and clearly outlaw it. Calling prisoners "dry and safe," and describing U.S. treatment of prisoners as "proper ... humane ... and appropriate," Rumsfeld has said that there was no doubt in his mind that the conditions of their captivity are "consistent with the Geneva Convention, for the most part." [37]

Rumsfeld and other spokespersons for the Bush administration do not speak on the record about specific activities, but they do acknowledge that the most aggressive interrogation techniques allowable by international standards are being employed. The commander of the coalition forces in Afghanistan, Daniel McNeill, said American tactics had been adapted to the situation, adding that "they are in accordance with what is generally accepted as interrogation techniques." [38]

Rendition

Another means of getting information from terrorists is the practice known as rendition. Rendition is the military practice of turning over, or rendering, arrestees for questioning by the authorities of another country. This practice differs from the formal legal process known as extradition, in which one country demands the return of a criminal held in custody by the civilian authorities of another country. Military renditions of terror suspects sometimes occur immediately upon arrest; others take place, usually secretly, at a later time if the suspect has not been cooperative under initial questioning.

Rendition of fugitive criminals has in the past been seen as a legitimate form of international cooperation, but some charge it is being used illegitimately in the war on terror. Groups such as Amnesty International and the Red Cross claim that its purpose is no longer to help other countries track down their own criminals, but to send terror suspects for interrogation in countries such as Egypt, Jordan, and Morocco, where torture of prisoners is known to occur. "We don't kick the [expletive] out of them. We send them to other countries so they can kick the [expletive] out of them," [39] one directly involved official is quoted by *Washington Post* reporters Priest and Gellman.

Any reports of mistreatment of a rendered suspect by CIA or other American operatives are classified, but according to one diplomat, "After September 11, these sorts of movements have been occurring all the time. It allows us to get information from terrorists in a way we can't do on American soil." [40] A senior U.S. official with direct knowledge of American interrogation practices summarized American involvement by saying, "In some cases involving interrogations in Saudi Arabia, we're able to observe directly through one-way mirrors the live investigations. In others we get summaries. We will feed questions to their investigators." But he adds, "They're still very much in control." [41]

It cannot be said with certainty how many suspects have been rendered during the war on terror because such transfers are usually made secretly, even of low-level operatives, and the circumstances of the custody of top terror suspects are rarely if ever revealed. However, some officials estimate that of the three thousand or so individuals in U.S. custody as terror suspects, approximately one hundred have already been rendered. Thousands more are believed to be in the custody of the foreign authorities who made the original arrest.

A Simmering Debate

The treatment of terror suspects is extremely controversial and depends on very different situations. For example, journalist Martin Edwin Andersen describes a situation in which "credible sources say a [detainee] has specific knowledge about a terrorist cell that has obtained a suitcase nuclear bomb and plans to use it within hours. . . . How can his captors . . . make him talk before it is too late?" [42] Some people argue that torture would be justified in such a situation, including well-known political commentator William F. Buckley: "We should not torture an al-Qaeda prisoner as a general rule. But to torture the one who knows where the hijacked airborne 737 is headed is an exemption to the rule." [43] Though the idea of torture is distasteful to many Americans, a few argue that it is time to establish laws permitting it under certain circumstances. "We can't

Harvard law professor Alan Dershowitz believes that torture should be permitted in certain cases.

just close our eyes and pretend we live in a pure world," [44] Harvard law professor Alan Dershowitz wrote in 2003, arguing that the war on terror requires a new legal process by which torture warrants can be granted to American authorities on a case-by-case basis.

Few topics generate more heated debate than the justification of torture. Most who argue openly for the selective use of torture feel it should be limited to situations in which crucial information is needed immediately to protect America and its people. However, experts point out that the information extracted under torture is often incorrect, blurted out simply to end the torture. Some suggest permitting the torture of suspected terrorists would have a deterrent effect, stopping people from becoming terrorists. Others counter that if the United States practices torture, American captives are more likely to be tortured by other nations in retaliation.

Some argue that torture is unacceptable under any circumstances, a violation of human dignity and human rights to which all people everywhere are entitled, regardless of what they have done. "We never want to become like those we claim as our enemies," [45] Scott Silliman, a professor at the Duke University law school, points out. Silliman speaks for many Americans who believe that their country does, and should always, set the standards for the world. Clearly the issue of treatment of terror suspects in detention will be a major test of American values as the war on terror proceeds.

Chapter Six

International Terrorists and the Law

Many terrorist suspects have been imprisoned for long periods without resolution of their cases in part because it is not clear what to do with them. In a conventional war, captured soldiers are supposed to be treated in accordance with clearly established international law and are to be released when the war is over. The war on terror, however, is unprecedented. Its means and battlefields are unconventional and its duration is uncertain. Consequently, the Bush administration is reluctant to rely solely on existing international law to determine the legal status of suspected terrorists in custody.

One of the most controversial issues of this new war is whether captives are entitled to be treated as POWs, prisoners of war. By law POWs are entitled to a minimum standard of care and certain legal rights that others captured during wartime are not entitled to receive. Another early concern, when an arrest occurs in a foreign country, is whether the accused will be tried there, moved to detention in another country, or brought back to the United States in a formal legal process known as extradition. Other complications revolve around what kind of trial they will receive, and what their punishment should be. In the new war on terror, most high-profile cases have not yet reached trial, so sentencing precedents have yet to be set. However, even without this last piece in play, the legal aspects of the war on terror have already proved to be extraordinarily complicated.

The Rights of POWs

The Geneva Conventions, developed after World War II, outline how those captured in war are to be treated. They make a distinction between captured soldiers and other prisoners. Soldiers acting under orders are considered to have been doing their job and are thus not to be punished for that by their captors. Instead, POWs are to be housed and fed in conditions equal to those of the soldiers of the country that captured them. They are required only to give identifying information about themselves. They are not to be mistreated for the purpose of extracting further information from them. They also cannot be tried for any acts they performed in connection with their legitimate duties as soldiers. They are entitled to visits and services of the International Red Cross, and once the war ends, they are to be released and sent home.

An Iraqi man caught robbing a bank loses his prosthetic leg in the scuffle. Because the war on terror is unprecedented, the legal status of suspects is difficult to determine.

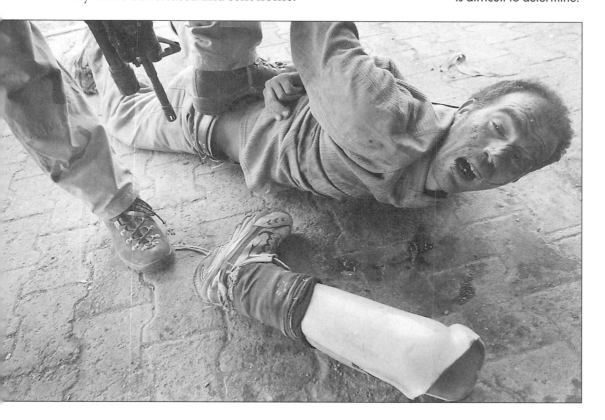

POW status is also extended to certain other combatants. In many parts of the world organized militias function in many respects as separate fighting forces allying themselves with national armies. Generally, a group that wears a uniform or other insignia easily identified at a distance, that takes orders from a clearly defined leadership, and that works on behalf of one or the other side in a conflict, has been considered entitled to POW status, even if its members are not soldiers in a government-sponsored army. So are civilians who fight against an invading army in immediate and direct defense of themselves, their families, and homes.

Those who take up arms for other purposes in a country at war, such as to loot or terrorize, are not considered entitled to the same rights as POWs. Though they have basic human rights, which include not being tortured, they are not entitled to any particular standard of housing or care, and they are also not entitled to visits by the Red Cross or other agencies to monitor their welfare. Interrogation does not have to stop if they refuse to offer information beyond basic identification, and they can continue to be held after hostilities cease.

The Guantánamo Bay Detainees

Most detainees at Guantánamo fall into one of three categories, but only a few neatly fit the Geneva Conventions division into POW and non-POW. The first group are soldiers serving in the army of the Taliban in Afghanistan.

Taliban soldiers were legitimate POWs during wartime, so under the Geneva Conventions, they should be released and sent home once hostilities end, unless sufficient evidence exists that they have committed war crimes. War crimes are acts disallowed for soldiers by international law, such as using hostages as human shields and other crimes such as theft or rape. If evidence of war crimes is brought against a POW, he may be kept in custody until he is brought to trial. However, all those held after the end of hostilities would have the same right as any other defendant to legal counsel, to know the specific charges

against them so that they could prepare a defense, and to a speedy trial. At this point this process is not in effect in any consistent way at Guantánamo Bay.

An al-Qaeda suspect wears a hood after the first session of his trial in Brussels, Belgium. Terrorist suspects apprehended outside Afghanistan are not considered POWs.

A second group consists of al-Qaeda members and other terrorists captured in Afghanistan and in other countries. Al-Qaeda members captured outside Afghanistan are not POWs in the sense that Taliban soldiers are, because they were not part of the Afghan war. Their incarceration is legal, just as it is for anyone suspected of a major crime, but they are not legitimately military prisoners and should not be kept in a military prison such as that at Guantánamo Bay. They are entitled to the same treatment as any other prisoner in the American judicial system, including being given an opportunity to talk to lawyers, hear the charges against them, and have a fair trial in a U.S. court. A third group consists of civilians, some of whom should probably not have been sent to Guantánamo Bay in the first place. They include street vendors, taxi drivers, and local farmers who were caught up in the mass arrests accompanying the fall of the Taliban. Others claim they were forced to fight by various means including threats to their families, and some reported being kidnapped and taken to army units. Afghan civilians caught up in mass arrest must be evaluated individually, to determine if there is legitimate reason to suspect them of any crime.

Prisoner Status, Prisoner Fate

Determining the legal status of each detainee is of utmost importance, but it has not yet occurred at Guantánamo Bay in part because precise legal definitions are hard to make. If all detainees were simply classified as POWs in the global war on terror (not just in a limited war in Afghanistan or Iraq), then they could according to the Geneva Conventions be held without charges until the war on terror was declared over, which is unlikely to occur for some time. Prolonged detention would not be a violation of their rights in this case. However, the Bush administration has not wanted to take this position for several reasons. First, POWs may legitimately refuse to answer questions, defeating the purpose of interrogation. As journalist Michael Elliott points out, "The whole point of the detention is to conduct interrogations and thus head off new acts of terrorism." [46] Second, if the detainees were simply fulfilling their duties as soldiers, even if this included shooting at American troops, they cannot be prosecuted for their acts, which is a goal of the Bush administration. The status of POW even for Taliban soldiers is troubling, despite the fact that under international law it is clearly appropriate. In the words of Harvard law professor Lawrence Tribe, "Releasing captured soldiers who belong to an enemy force committed to the murder of American civilians [would be] suicide." [47]

Part of the problem is that the current war on terrorism does not fit easily into the framework considered by the authors of the Geneva Conventions. The Bush administration has thus felt it necessary to amend some generally accepted international obligations. For example, the Geneva Conventions are very clear that a determination of whether a detainee is or is not a POW must be made promptly, and by an independent and impartial tribunal, which in this case presumably would be an American court. Instead, Secretary of Defense Donald Rumsfeld announced that the Guantánamo Bay detainees did not meet the criteria for POW status, and as "unlawful" or "enemy combatants" they "do not have any rights under the Geneva Conventions."[48] The terms "unlawful combatant" and "enemy combatant" are not defined under the conventions, which specify that all detainees must fall into one of the convention categories, and also assert that all categories are afforded certain essential rights.

Iraqi POWs wait to be released from a U.S. military camp in southern Iraq.

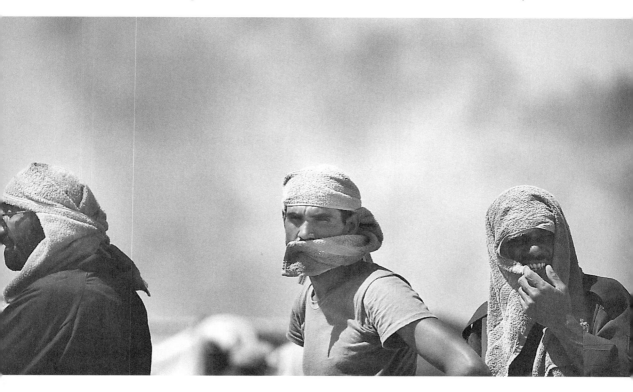

The international legal community not only has rejected the Bush administration's analysis of the situation, but has argued that this matter is not Rumsfeld's or Bush's to decide in the first place. It is up to a judge to decide, who must do so based on the evidence in each detainee's case. There would probably be very little disagreement that a known al-Qaeda member should be kept in custody even if concrete evidence of actual criminal behavior on his part is lacking. However, as *Atlantic Monthly* writer Stuart Taylor Jr. points out, the problem with the handling of terrorism suspects to date is the Bush administration's "refusal to acknowledge any obligation to produce any evidence at all linking [suspects] to al-Qaeda."[49]

Extradition

Since the end of the military action in Afghanistan, arrests of suspected terrorists have continued around the world, though on a much smaller scale. Some arrestees have been brought to Guantánamo Bay, but others have been transferred to various countries in a process called extradition. Extradition is the means by which a person suspected of a crime is delivered through a formal legal process to the country in which, or against which, the crime was committed. In other words, if a Canadian committed a murder in Canada and was arrested in the United States, he or she would be returned to Canada to face trial and punishment. The United States has signed extradition treaties with more than a hundred countries.

Several factors make extraditing terror suspects to the United States difficult. One is that many countries have abolished the death penalty, and thus are unwilling to hand over terror suspects for trial in the United States if they might face capital punishment. In the case of high-profile terrorists, especially those associated with September 11, the United States is unwilling to rule out the death penalty. If, for example, Osama bin Laden were captured in another country, the U.S. government would be extremely reluctant to agree in advance not to seek the death penalty even if that was the only way to bring him to trial on U.S. soil.

An additional difficulty is that different governments define political crimes differently. A person who carries out a bombing designed to overthrow a repressive government will likely be considered a criminal by that government. Other countries, however, might consider that act legitimate rebellion against tyranny. If countries cannot mutually agree that a crime has been committed, extradition will not occur. This is likely to become an increasingly important issue for the United States. If, for example, an Iraqi attacks an American military base in occupied Iraq, then escapes into another country, it is not clear how that other country might view that action. There is an honorable tradition of fighting the foreign occupation of one's country, and one man's terrorist is another man's freedom fighter. The international unpopularity of American foreign policy regarding the war on terrorism makes it likely that this issue will dominate international discussions in the months and years to come.

Terrorists in the Federal Courts

Regardless of these difficulties, the fact remains that there are many terror suspects in American custody and something must eventually be done about each one. Each suspect will experience at least one of three things: release, trial, or continued detention. Those who are eventually prosecuted for criminal acts will face trial in one of three legal venues: U.S. federal courts, military legal proceedings, or the judicial system of the country where the crime was committed. The latter is unlikely for most detainees, because the United States wants to retain greater control over the process.

Prosecution in a federal court has been selected for all American citizens accused of crimes of terrorism because it

A Northern Alliance soldier escorts John Walker Lindh, an American who was captured fighting for the Taliban.

affords the broadest rights during trial and on appeal. John Walker Lindh, a young American who was captured fighting with the Taliban, is serving a twenty-year sentence as a result of a plea bargain in federal court. He pleaded guilty to one count of supplying services to the Taliban and another charge of carrying weapons while fighting against the American-backed Northern Alliance in Afghanistan. Another American citizen, Jose Padilla, is being held in military detention in South Carolina after his arrest in Chicago on a terrorism charge, and Yaser Hamdi, another American citizen, was captured in Afghanistan and is being held in military custody in

Virginia. Both are likely to be tried eventually by federal courts.

The federal courts have also been chosen as the appropriate judicial venue for certain noncitizens. Richard Reid, a British citizen, pleaded guilty in late 2002 to eight charges including attempted murder and attempted use of a weapon of mass destruction, in connection with his plan to destroy an American Airlines passenger jet in midflight with explosives concealed in his shoe. In U.S. federal court he was given three life sentences and additional time for other related crimes—a total of 110 years—so as to remove any possibility for future parole. In spring 2003 the case against accused al-Qaeda member Zacarias Moussaoui was being prepared in federal court in

While a passenger on board an American Airlines transatlantic flight, Richard Reid attempted to detonate explosives hidden in his shoes.

Alexandria, Virginia, on a number of charges relating to his alleged role in the events of September 11.

Military Courts and Tribunals

Military courts are also being considered as an option for other terror suspects. In a military court, the verdict is rendered not by a panel of citizens but by a few military officers. The Bush administration favors this venue for foreign terror suspects because it limits the rights of the accused to legal counsel and to appeals of convictions, and thus can be very quick and efficient. Moreover, such trials can be conducted with a minimum of publicity and limited disclosure of evidence to the defendant.

Even more streamlined is the military tribunal, whose use Bush authorized in November 2001 for the express purpose of trying terrorists. In a tribunal, a panel of officers convenes on the spot to make prompt and usually final decisions in cases such as desertion or war crimes. Tribunals originated as a way of settling matters in the midst of battle, where lengthy trials or convening a full military court is impractical.

Both types of military procedure are of concern to many legal experts. According to reporter Gina Holland, "Under either system, military officers would determine the fate of war crimes suspects. Their authority would even allow imposition of death sentences."[50] According to Amnesty International, the tribunals authorized by Bush "would flout international fair trial standards and have the power to hand down death sentences with no right of appeal,"[51] by a vote of only two-thirds of the panel. So far, no tribunals have actually been convened to deal with terrorists. Contrary to alarmist predictions, their proceedings are likely to be consistent with international law and with the human rights that are at the core of the American concept of justice.

No Easy Answers

Journalist Stuart Taylor summarizes the analyses of many scholars and other observers in saying, "These are difficult

U.S. attorney general John Ashcroft holds an al-Qaeda handbook as he testifies before the U.S. Senate Judiciary Committee on behalf of the use of military tribunals.

cases for which our legal system was not designed."[52] The difficulties begin long before any selection of courtroom is made, and even before an individual is formally charged.

The architects of American and international law did not anticipate a war such as the one declared by the Bush administration. Effectively waging war on terrorists means employing controversial practices that potentially under-mine fundamental civil liberties. The challenge lies in ensur-ing, in the words of journalist Taylor, that "the war against terrorism [does] not become a war against due process of law."[53] The United States has always positioned itself as a champion of human rights and the rule of law, and the world is watching to see how it will live up to its own standards in the current situation. A war without borders, without an opposing army, and without a clearly achievable objective by which victory could be declared may be as necessary as any other war, but it presents ethical as well as practical chal-lenges the United States and the rest of the world have only begun to address.

Notes

Introduction: A War Without Borders

1. George W. Bush, "Address to a Joint Session of Congress and the American People," September 20, 2001, White House. www.whitehouse.gov.

2. Bush, "Address to a Joint Session of Congress and the American People."

3. Gore Vidal, *Perpetual War for Perpetual Peace: How We Got to Be So Hated.* New York: Thunder's Mouth Press, 2002.

4. Bush, "Address to a Joint Session of Congress and the American People."

Chapter 1: The Role of the Military

5. Johanna McGeary, "Hunting Osama," *Time,* December 10, 2001, Time Online Edition. www.time.com.

6. Quoted in McGeary, "Hunting Osama."

7. Quoted in Mark Mazzetti, "On the Ground," February 25, 2002, USNews.com. www.usnews.com.

8. Quoted in Richard LaCayo, "The Quest for Fugitives," *Time,* January 6, 2002, Time Online Edition. www.time.com.

9. George W. Bush, "State of the Union Address," January 29, 2002, White House. www.whitehouse.gov.

Chapter 2: The Covert War Against International Terror

10. Bush, "Address to a Joint Session of Congress and the American People."

11. James Risen, "CIA Names Agent Killed in Fortress," *New York Times,* November 29, 2001.

12. Mazzetti, "On the Ground."

13. Mazzetti, "On the Ground."

14. Robin Moore, *The Hunt for Bin Laden: Task Force Dagger*. New York: Random House, 2003, p. xx.

15. Douglas Waller, "The CIA's Secret Army," *Time,* February 3, 2003.

16. Waller, "The CIA's Secret Army."

17. Waller, "The CIA's Secret Army."

18. Quoted in Waller, "The CIA's Secret Army."

19. Samuel M. Katz, *Relentless Pursuit: The DSS and the Manhunt for the Al-Qaeda Terrorists.* New York: Tom Doherty, 2002, p. 15.

Chapter 3: The Technological War on Terror

20. "Hunt for bin Laden Goes Online," July 23, 2002, CNN.com. www.cnn.com.

21. Quoted in Daniel Sieberg, "Bin Laden Exploits Technology to Suit His Needs," September 21, 2001, CNN.com. www.cnn.com.

22. Sieberg, "Bin Laden Exploits Technology to Suit His Needs."

23. Quoted in Sieberg, "Bin Laden Exploits Technology to Suit His Needs."

24. Quoted in Sieberg, "Bin Laden Exploits Technology to Suit His Needs."

25. Elizabeth Weise, "Surveillance Casts an Eye to the Future," July 23, 2002, USA Today Online. www.usatoday.com.

26. Lawyers Committee for Human Rights, *A Year of Loss: Reexamining Civil Liberties Since September 11.* New York: Lawyers Committee for Human Rights, 2002, p. 22.

27. Quoted in Lawyers Committee for Human Rights, *A Year of Loss,* p. 7.

28. Quoted in Lawyers Committee for Human Rights, *A Year of Loss,* p. 7.

Chapter 4: Winning Global Support to Fight Terror

29. Bush, "Address to a Joint Session of Congress and the American People."

30. Quoted in Johanna McGeary, "Next Stop Mindanao," *Time,* January 28, 2002, Time Online Edition. www.time.com.

Chapter 5: International Terrorists in Custody

31. Richard Phillips, "New Revelations About Guantanamo Bay Prisoners," March 30, 2003, Jeff Rense Program. www.rense.com.

32. Quoted in "Guantanamo Suicide Attempts Probed," *New York Times,* March 4, 2003. www.nytimes.com.

33. Dana Priest and Barton Gellman, "For CIA Suspects Abroad, Brass-Knuckle Treatment," *Washington Post,* December 27, 2002. www.washingtonpost.com.

34. Priest and Gellman, "For CIA Suspects Abroad, Brass-Knuckle Treatment."

35. U.S. Department of State, "Initial Report of the United States of America to the UN Committee Against Torture," October 15, 1999.

36. Human Rights Watch, "The Legal Prohibition Against Torture," *Human Rights Watch Backgrounder,* March 11, 2003. www.hrw.org.

37. Quoted in Alexandra Poulos, "Treatment of Prisoners at Guantanamo May Injure U.S.-British Alliance," January 21, 2002, Radio Free Europe. www.rferl.org.

38. Quoted in Duncan Campbell, "Afghans Die After Beatings at U.S. Base," *Age,* March 8, 2003. www.theage.com.au.

39. Quoted in Priest and Gellman, "For CIA Suspects Abroad, Brass-Knuckle Treatment."

40. Quoted in "Rendition, Torture, Other Forms of Unlawful Interrogation," March 9, 2002, Center for Cooperative Research. www.cooperativeresearch.org.

41. Quoted in Priest and Gellman, "For CIA Suspects Abroad, Brass-Knuckle Treatment."

42. Martin Edwin Andersen, "Is Torture an Option in the War on Terror?" *Insight,* April 1, 2003. www.insightmag.com.

43. Quoted in Andersen, "Is Torture an Option in the War on Terror?"

44. Quoted in Andersen, "Is Torture an Option in the War on Terror?"

45. Quoted in Jodie Morse, "How Do We Make Him Talk?" *Time*, April 15, 2002, Time Online Edition. www.time.com.

Chapter 6: International Terrorists and the Law

46. Michael Elliott, "Welcome to Camp X-Ray," *Time*, January 28, 2002, Time Online Edition. www.time.com.

47. Quoted in Stuart Taylor Jr., "Maybe the Military Should Have Kept John Walker Lindh," June 25, 2002, Atlantic Online. www.theatlantic.com.

48. Quoted in "Background Paper on Geneva Conventions and Persons Held by U.S. Forces," *Human Rights Watch Press Backgrounder,* January 29, 2002, Human Rights Watch. www.hrw.org.

49. Taylor, "Maybe the Military Should Have Kept John Walker Lindh."

50. Gina Holland, "U.S. Readies Iraq War-Crimes Prosecutions," *Compuserve News,* March 30, 2003. www.compuserve.com.

51. "Detainees in Guantanamo Bay Should Not Be Beyond the Protection of the Law," *Amnesty International Public Statement,* December 13, 2002, Amnesty International. www.amnesty.org.

52. Taylor, "Maybe the Military Should Have Kept John Walker Lindh."

53. Taylor, "Maybe the Military Should Have Kept John Walker Lindh."

For Further Reading

Books

Ron Fridell, *Spying: The Modern World of Espionage*. Brookfield, CT: Millbrook, 2002. Thorough and exciting discussion of the world of spies.

Jan Goldberg, *The Green Berets: The U.S. Army Special Forces*. New York: Rosen, 2003. Up-to-date book about becoming and serving as a Green Beret.

Nate Hardcastle, *American Soldier: Stories of Special Forces from Iraq to Afghanistan*. New York: Thunder's Mouth, 2002. A collection of memoirs from commandos, SEALs, and others involved in Special Forces operations in recent years.

Robert C. Kennedy, *Life in the Army Special Forces*. New York: Scholastic Library, 2000. Good general discussion of the work of the Special Forces around the world.

Elaine Landau, *Osama bin Laden: A War Against the West*. Brookfield, CT: Millbrook, 2002. Biographical and other background information on the world's most wanted person.

Lawrence P. Pringle, *Chemical and Biological Warfare: The Cruelest Weapons*. Berkeley Heights, NJ: Enslow, 2000. Discusses the development and potential threat of chemical and biological weapons of mass destruction.

Charles W. Sasser, *Encyclopedia of the Navy SEALs*. New York: Facts On File, 2002. Thorough reference on all aspects of the operation of the U.S. Navy SEALs.

Douglas C. Waller, *Commandos: The Inside Story of America's Secret Soldiers*. New York: Dell, 1994. A best-selling book about the training and use of commandos.

Ralph Edward Weber, *Spymasters: Ten CIA Officials in Their Own Words*. Wilmington, DE: Scholarly Resources, 1998. Interesting and lively insider discussion of life in the CIA.

Donna Koren Wells and Bruce C. Morris, *Live Aware Not in Fear: A Teen Culture Shift for Our Challenging Time.* Health Communications, 2002. An excellent source of information for teens worried about terrorism and its personal and global impact.

Alex Woolf, *Osama bin Laden.* Minneapolis: Lerner, 2003. Good basic biography of the leader of al-Qaeda.

Websites

Amnesty International (www.amnesty.org). The website of the premier organization monitoring human rights around the world.

Center for Cooperative Research (www.cooperativeresearch.org). An excellent source of summaries of a variety of important political issues, presented in an easy-to-read format.

Central Intelligence Agency (www.cia.gov). This site provides good information on the structure, leadership, and activities of the CIA in relation to counterterrorism and other matters.

Federal Bureau of Investigation (www.fbi.gov). This sites provides general information about the FBI with articles about subjects relating to counterterrorism.

Human Rights Watch (www.hrw.org). The website of the global human rights organization.

Radio Free Europe (www.rferl.org). The website of one of the oldest and most respected international radio news sources.

Time (www.time.com). One of the world's premier weekly magazines provides current and archived issues online.

US News (www.USnews.com). The website of another influential weekly magazine.

USA Today (www.usatoday.com). Good for quick summaries of breaking news in the war on terror.

Washington Post (www.washingtonpost.com). The website of a newspaper famous for its exposés of current issues.

White House (www.whitehouse.gov). The website operated by the president's office.

Works Consulted

Books

Yonah Alexander, *Combating Terrorism: Strategies of Ten Countries.* Ann Arbor: University of Michigan Press, 2002. A thorough discussion of the efforts of ten countries, including the United States, to combat terrorism.

Robert Baer, *See No Evil: The True Story of a Ground Soldier in the CIA's War on Terrorism.* New York: Three Rivers, 2002. Best-selling book discussing the shortcomings of the CIA before September 11 and the implications for the war on terror today.

Daniel Benjamin and Steven Simon, *The Age of Sacred Terror.* New York: Random House, 2002. Thorough discussion of the rise of Islamic fundamentalism and its significance to the war on terror.

Noam Chomsky, *9-11.* New York: Seven Stories, 2001. An early, highly acclaimed short work about the significance of September 11 and the American reaction.

Samuel M. Katz, *Relentless Pursuit: The DSS and the Manhunt for the Al-Qaeda Terrorists.* New York: Tom Doherty, 2002. Detailed discussion of the DSS role in the search for al-Qaeda terrorists threatening diplomatic personnel abroad.

Lawyers Committee for Human Rights, *A Year of Loss: Reexamining Civil Liberties Since September 11.* New York: Lawyers Committee for Human Rights, 2002. A human rights advocacy group discusses the various bills passed since September 11 and their effect on civil liberties.

Bernard Lewis, *What Went Wrong.* Oxford, England: Oxford University Press, 2002. An acclaimed discussion of the roots of the hostility of the Muslim world toward the West.

Robin Moore, *The Hunt for Bin Laden: Task Force Dagger.* New York: Random House, 2003. A thorough discussion of the Afghan campaign to find Osama bin Laden.

Roger Scruton, *The West and the Rest.* Wilmington, DE: Intercollegiate Studies Institute, 2002. A discussion of globalism and its role in the mounting anti-American sentiment at the heart of many terrorist acts.

Gore Vidal, *Perpetual War for Perpetual Peace: How We Got to Be So Hated.* New York: Thunder's Mouth Press, 2002. A discussion of the role of the United States in global politics and its connection to the rise of anti-American terrorism.

Howard Zinn, *Terrorism and War.* New York: Seven Stories, 2002. Short work by a controversial American historian about American tactics against terrorism and growing American dissent.

Periodicals

"How Do US Interrogators Make a Captured Terrorist Talk?" *Wall Street Journal,* March 4, 2003.

James Risen, "CIA Names Agent Killed in Fortress," *New York Times,* November 29, 2001.

Bill Saporito and Tim McGirk, "Architect of Terror," *Time,* March 10, 2003.

John Schwartz and John Mintz, "Chipping Away at a Fundamental Freedom," *Washington Post,* March 4, 1994, p. F1.

U.S. Department of State, "Initial Report of the United States of America to the UN Committee Against Torture," October 15, 1999.

Douglas Waller, "The CIA's Secret Army," *Time,* February 3, 2003.

Internet Sources

Martin Edwin Andersen, "Is Torture an Option in the War on Terror?" *Insight,* April 1, 2003. www.insightmag.com.

"Background Paper on Geneva Conventions and Persons Held by U.S. Forces," *Human Rights Watch Press Backgrounder,* January 29, 2002, Human Rights Watch. www.hrw.org.

George W. Bush, "Address to a Joint Session of Congress and the American People," September 20, 2001, White House. www.white house.gov.

———, "State of the Union Address," January 29, 2002, White House. www.whitehouse.gov.

Duncan Campbell, "Afghans Die After Beatings at U.S. Base," *Age*, March 8, 2003. www.theage.com.au.

———, "US Interrogators Turn to 'Torture Lite.'" *Guardian*, January 25, 2003. www.guardian.co.uk

"Detainees in Guantanamo Bay Should Not Be Beyond the Protection of the Law," *Amnesty International Public Statement*, December 13, 2002, Amnesty International. www.amnesty.org.

Michael Elliott, "Welcome to Camp X-Ray," *Time*, January 28, 2002, Time Online Edition. www.time.com.

"Guantanamo Suicide Attempts Probed," *New York Times*, March 4, 2003. www.nytimes.com.

Gina Holland, "U.S. Readies Iraq War-Crimes Prosecutions," *Compuserve News*, March 30, 2003. www.compuserve.com.

Reyko Huang, "South Asia and the United States Assessing New Policies and Old Programs." *CDI Terrorism Project*, May 24, 2002, CDI.www.cdi.org.

Human Rights Watch, "The Legal Prohibition Against Torture," *Human Rights Watch Backgrounder*, March 11, 2003. www.hrw.org.

"Hunt for bin Laden Goes Online," July 23, 2002, CNN.com. www.cnn.com.

Karen Kaplan, "Securing the Future," *Los Angeles Times*, September 20, 2001. www.latimes.com.

Jamey Keaton, "US Nabs Suspected Rebels in Afghanistan," *Compuserve News*, March 25, 2003. compuserve.com.

Richard LaCayo, "The Quest for Fugitives," *Time*, January 6, 2002, Time Online Edition. www.time.com.

Mark Mazzetti, "On the Ground," February 25, 2002, USNews.com. www.usnews.com.

Johanna McGeary, "Hunting Osama," *Time*, December 10, 2001, Time Online Edition. www.time.com.

————, "Next Stop Mindanao," *Time*, January 28, 2002, Time Online Edition. www.time.com.

Tim McGirk, "Anatomy of a Raid," *Time*, April 15, 2002, Time Online Edition. www.time.com.

Michael Moran, "Hunt or Wild Goose Chase?" MSNBC, December 19, 2001. www.msnbc.com.

Jodie Morse, "How Do We Make Him Talk?" *Time*, April 15, 2002, Time Online Edition. www.time.com.

David Pace, "Moussaoui Wants Testimony of Suspects," *Compuserve News*, March 21, 2003, www.compuserve.com

"Pakistan's Net." *Washington Times*, March 21, 2003. www.washington times.com.

Richard Phillips, "New Revelations About Guantanamo Bay Prisoners," March 30, 2003, Jeff Rense Program. www.rense.com.

Alexandra Poulos, "Treatment of Prisoners at Guantanamo May Injure U.S.-British Alliance," January 21, 2002, Radio Free Europe. www.rferl.org.

Dana Priest and Barton Gellman, "For CIA Suspects Abroad, Brass-Knuckle Treatment," *Washington Post*, December 27, 2002. www.washingtonpost.com.

"Rendition, Torture, Other Forms of Unlawful Interrogation," March 9, 2002, Center for Cooperative Research. www.cooperativeresearch.org.

Muddassir Rizvi, "Pakistan's Dilemma: Cooperating with US Could Spark Rebellion," September 14, 2001, www.imdiversity.com.

Alex Salkever, "The Intensifying Scrutiny at Airports," June 5, 2002. Business Week Online. www.businessweek.com.

Daniel Sieberg, "Bin Laden Exploits Technology to Suit His Needs," September 21, 2001, CNN.com. www.cnn.com.

Stuart Taylor Jr., "Maybe the Military Should Have Kept John Walker Lindh," June 25, 2002, Atlantic Online. www.theatlantic.com.

"Technology Aids Hunt for Terrorists." *Computerworld*, September 9, 2002. www.computerworld.com.

Simon Tisdall, "US Aims Its Sights on Philippines," *Guardian*, January 24, 2002. www.guardian.co.uk.

Elizabeth Weise, "Surveillance Casts an Eye to the Future," July 23, 2002, USA Today Online. www.usatoday.com.

Index

Picture Credits

Cover Photo: © Getty Images
© AFP, 20
© AFP/CORBIS, 23, 25, 26, 55, 56, 62, 67, 73, 89
© AP/Wide World Photos, 15, 28, 31, 33, 35, 36, 38, 39, 43, 44, 49, 60, 61, 79
© CORBIS, 47
© CORBIS SYGMA, 11
© Landov, 32, 42, 68, 70, 71, 81, 83, 86, 87
© James Leynse/CORBIS, 50
© Wally McNamee/CORBIS, 76
© Reuters NewMedia Inc./CORBIS, 18

About the Author

Laurel Corona lives in Lake Arrowhead, California, and teaches English and humanities at San Diego City College. She has a master's degree from the University of Chicago and a Ph.D. from the University of California at Davis. Dr. Corona has written many other books for Lucent Books, including *Life in Moscow, Poland, France, Israel,* and *The World Trade Center.*

Sometimes
Mama and Papa Fight

Sometimes
Mama and Papa Fight

by
Marjorie Weinman Sharmat

pictures by Kay Chorao

Harper & Row, Publishers

07

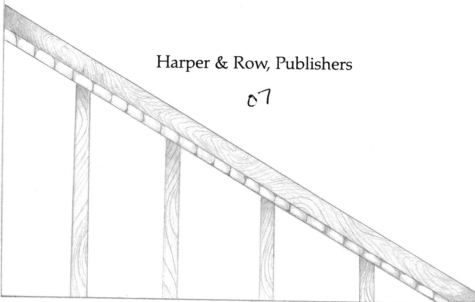

Library of Congress Cataloging in Publication Data
Sharmat, Marjorie Weinman.
Sometimes Mama and Papa fight.

SUMMARY: Kevin and his sister realize that
fights, even between parents, can be a natural
part of life in a family.
[1. Quarreling—Fiction.   2. Family life—
Fiction] I. Chorao, Kay.   II. Title.
PZ7.S5299Sm   1980   [E]   79-2018
ISBN 0-06-025611-7
ISBN 0-06-025612-5 lib. bdg.

for Betty of Oakdale Street —M.W.S.

for Keir Buckhurst and Jane Kelvin —K.C.

ometimes
Mama and Papa fight.
They're doing it now.
My sister Millicent and I put our hands
over our ears.
But we can still hear them.
"It's your fault!" Mama is shouting.
"No, it's not. It's yours!" Papa
is shouting back.

Mama's face is very white.
Papa is waving his hands around.
I hate it when they look so mad.
I'm scared.
I wish I could go to school,
and then the fight would be
all finished when I got home.
But it's Sunday.

I'm thinking about something else now.
I'm thinking about a striped mouse,
because that's a funny thing
and not like a fight.

Now I'm making up a song and
singing it, and Millicent is singing it, too.
La-la-la
la-la-la.
We can't hear the fight over our singing.

Most days Mama and Papa like
each other and love each other.
Some days Mama hums.
She hums off-key, but I like it.
And Papa whistles.
Papa's a good whistler.
They hum and whistle together.
They sound nice.

I wish I could say,
"Hey, Mama. Hey, Papa. That's a
silly fight you're having, so stop
that silly fight."
And if they don't stop, I wish
I could say, "Stop this instant!!"
just like they say to Millicent and me
when we fight.
Maybe they'll ask me to choose sides.
What'll I do?

Maybe I'll tell them I don't
feel good.
Maybe I'll say I'm hot and have
a stomachache.
Then they'll think about me
and not about them.
Papa will cook me something special
and Mama will put me to bed.
And they'll both keep coming to my
room to take care of me.

I remember when they had
another fight.
There was a new chair.
And Mama said, "It's beautiful."
But Papa said, "It's ugly."
And then they were talking louder
and shouting.
Millicent and I were drawing pictures.
I pressed down so hard
I broke my pencil.

I ran to them.

I wanted to make that fight stop.

But I didn't know how.

"Oh, Kevin!" Papa said, and he
hugged me.

So did Mama.

"Is it all over?" I asked. "Is it?"

"All over," said Papa.

"I hate fights," I said.

"So do we," said Mama.

"But they happen sometimes," she said.
"And then they get over with.
That's the way it is with fights."
I leaned against Mama and Papa
and they felt big and warm
and it was nice.
Then Millicent came
with our drawings.

"Let's try a picture,"
Mama said to Papa.
And they sat down and drew
some pictures.
"You draw funny," I said.
We all laughed.
And everything was okay again.

It's quiet now.
Somebody's coming up the stairs.
"Mama! Papa!"

Millicent and I run to them.
They swoop us up
and swing us around
and swing us around.

It's dizzy and silly.
"Oh, it's over!
That fight's gone!"
I ask them to swing me around again,
and they do.